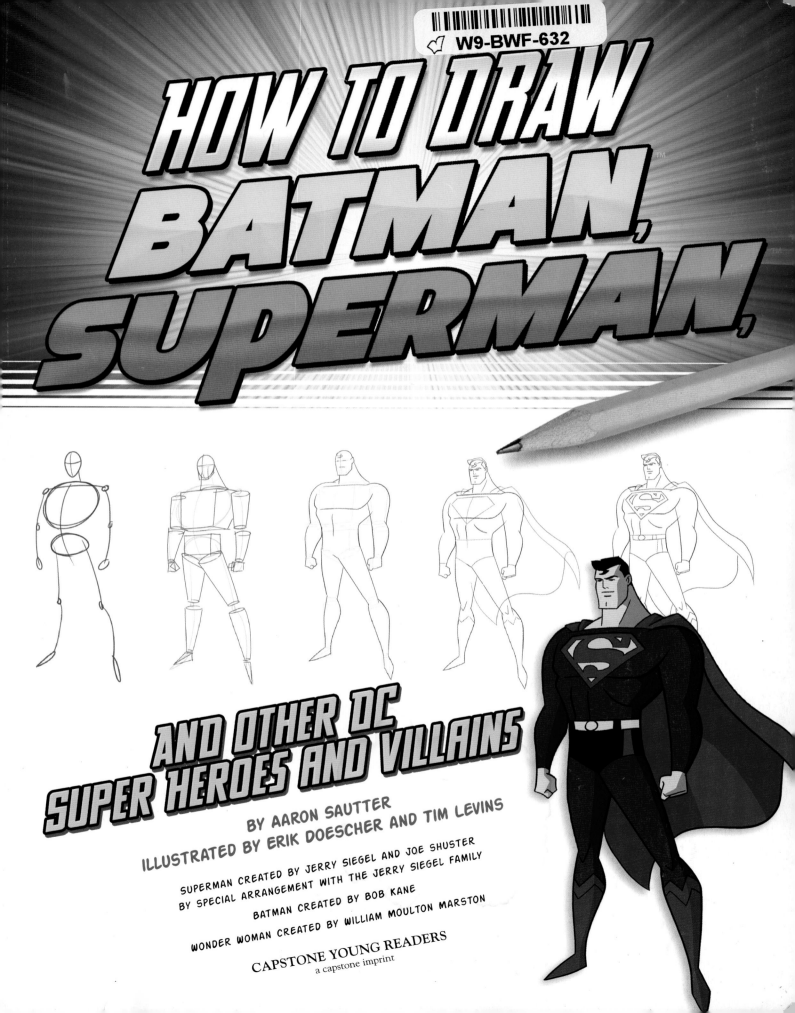

HOW TO DRAW BATMAN, SUPERMAN,

AND OTHER DC SUPER HEROES AND VILLAINS

BY AARON SAUTTER

ILLUSTRATED BY ERIK DOESCHER AND TIM LEVINS

SUPERMAN CREATED BY JERRY SIEGEL AND JOE SHUSTER
BY SPECIAL ARRANGEMENT WITH THE JERRY SIEGEL FAMILY

BATMAN CREATED BY BOB KANE

WONDER WOMAN CREATED BY WILLIAM MOULTON MARSTON

CAPSTONE YOUNG READERS
a capstone imprint

TABLE OF CONTENTS

LET'S DRAW INCREDIBLE DC SUPER HEROES AND VILLAINS!

The forces of evil are on the move and villains are plotting to take over the world. Who can people turn to in this dark hour? Super heroes!

Do you enjoy seeing Batman outwit the Joker? Do you like watching Superman defeat Lex Luthor's evil plans? Maybe you enjoy stories about Wonder Woman, Green Lantern, and The Flash as they defend the Earth. Or maybe you just enjoy rooting against bad guys like Sinestro, Cheetah, Black Manta, or Captain Cold.

The DC Universe is filled with hundreds of colorful heroes and villains—and now you can draw your favorites! This book is packed with fun drawing projects to get you started. Want to draw Superman and his Fortress of Solitude? Want to draw Batman and his Batmobile? Those are here, along with dozens of other super heroes and their foes!

What are you waiting for? Gather your supplies and sharpen your pencils. Then turn the page and start sketching your favorite DC Super Heroes and Super-Villains!

WHAT YOU'LL NEED

YOU DON'T NEED SUPERPOWERS TO DRAW MIGHTY HEROES AND SINISTER VILLAINS. BUT YOU'LL NEED SOME BASIC TOOLS. GATHER THE FOLLOWING SUPPLIES BEFORE STARTING YOUR AWESOME ART.

PAPER: You can get special drawing paper from art supply and hobby stores. But any type of blank, unlined paper will work fine.

PENCILS: Drawings should always be done in pencil first. Even the pros use them. If you make a mistake, it'll be easy to erase and redo it. Keep plenty of these essential drawing tools on hand.

PENCIL SHARPENER: To make clean lines, you need to keep your pencils sharp. Get a good pencil sharpener. You'll use it a lot.

ERASERS: As you draw, you're sure to make mistakes. Erasers give artists the power to turn back time and erase those mistakes. Get some high quality rubber or kneaded erasers. They'll last a lot longer than pencil erasers.

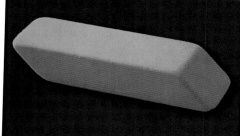

MARKER PENS: When your drawing is ready, trace over the final lines with black marker pen. The dark lines will help make your characters stand out on the page.

COLORED PENCILS AND MARKERS: Ready to finish your masterpiece? Bring your characters to life and give them some color with colored pencils or markers.

CHAPTER 1
SUPERMAN

Some people call him the Last Son of Krypton or the Man of Steel. But whatever people call him, one thing remains true—Superman is the first and most powerful super hero of them all.

Superman was born as Kal-El on the planet Krypton. However, he didn't grow up there. His parents, Jor-El and Lara Lor-Van, knew that Krypton was about to be destroyed. To save their baby son, they sent him to Earth in a special spacecraft. When young Kal landed near Smallville, Kansas, he was found by Jonathan and Martha Kent. The loving couple named him Clark and raised him as their own son.

As Clark grew he learned that he had many amazing abilities. Earth's yellow sun gave him powers such as super-strength and speed, heat vision, flight, and bulletproof skin. As an adult Clark chose to use his powers to defend the Earth and protect its people. He became Superman, the Man of Steel!

Welcome to the world of Superman! Grab your pencils and get ready to begin sketching Superman, his friends, and several of his most powerful enemies.

Let your imagination soar and see what kind of Superman drawings you can create yourself!

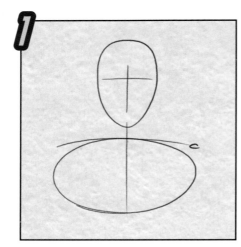

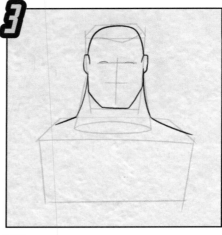

CLARK KENT

When not fighting villains as Superman, Clark Kent works as a mild-mannered reporter at the *Daily Planet* newspaper. Clark chose to become a reporter so that he could be close by when the people of Metropolis need him.

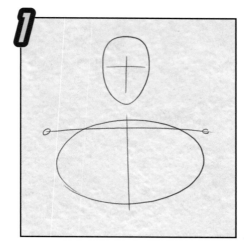

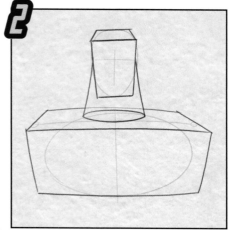

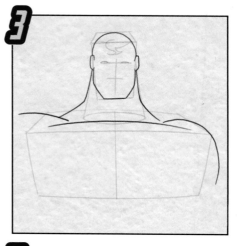

SUPERMAN

When a threat arises in the city, Clark quickly changes into the Man of Steel to deal with it head-on. Superman closely guards his secret identity. Only a few people know that Superman earns a living writing news stories for the *Daily Planet*.

SUPERMAN'S SUIT

When Clark arrived on Earth from Krypton, he was wrapped in blue and red blankets. Martha Kent used the blankets to create Superman's suit and cape. The Man of Steel doesn't wear a mask with his outfit. He wants to earn people's trust and show that he has nothing to hide.

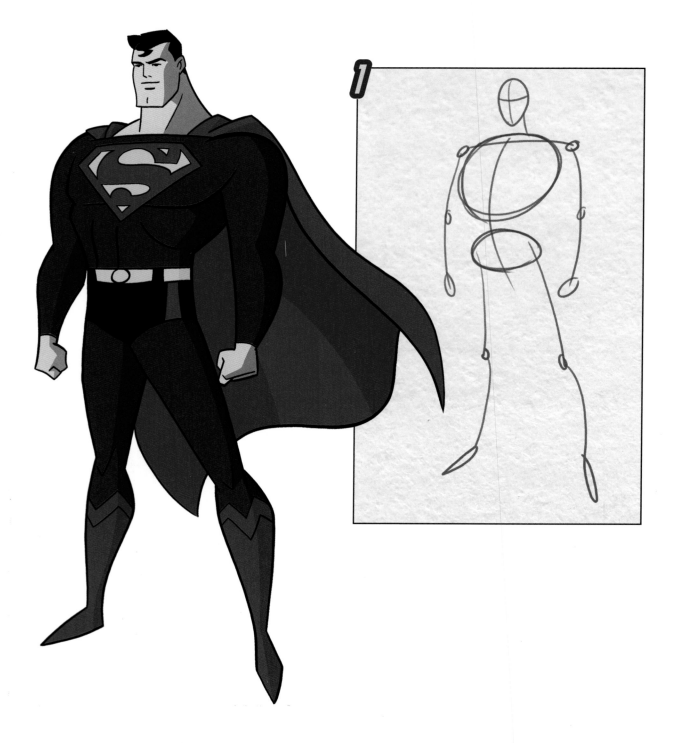

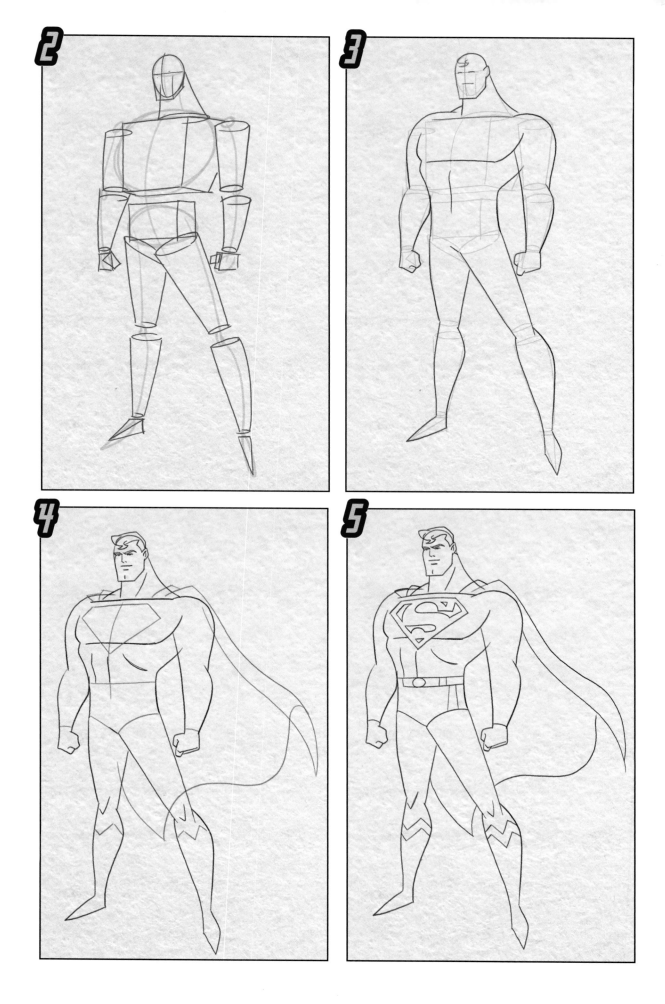

FORTRESS OF SOLITUDE

Superman normally calls Metropolis home. But when he needs time to himself, he goes to his secret Fortress of Solitude in the Arctic. There is only one door into the fortress, which is always locked. Only Superman has the strength needed to lift the giant metal key that unlocks the fortress door.

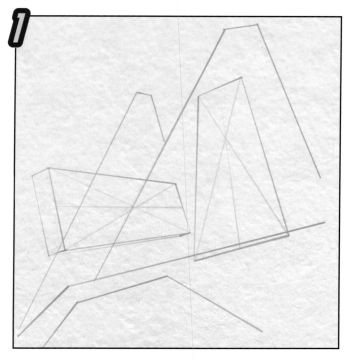

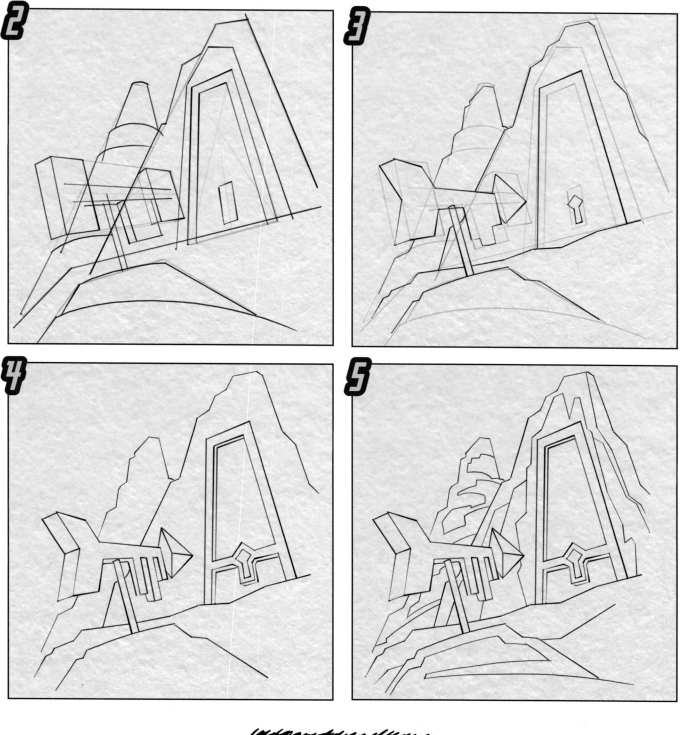

DRAWING IDEA
Next try to draw Superman lifting the key to open the Fortress door!

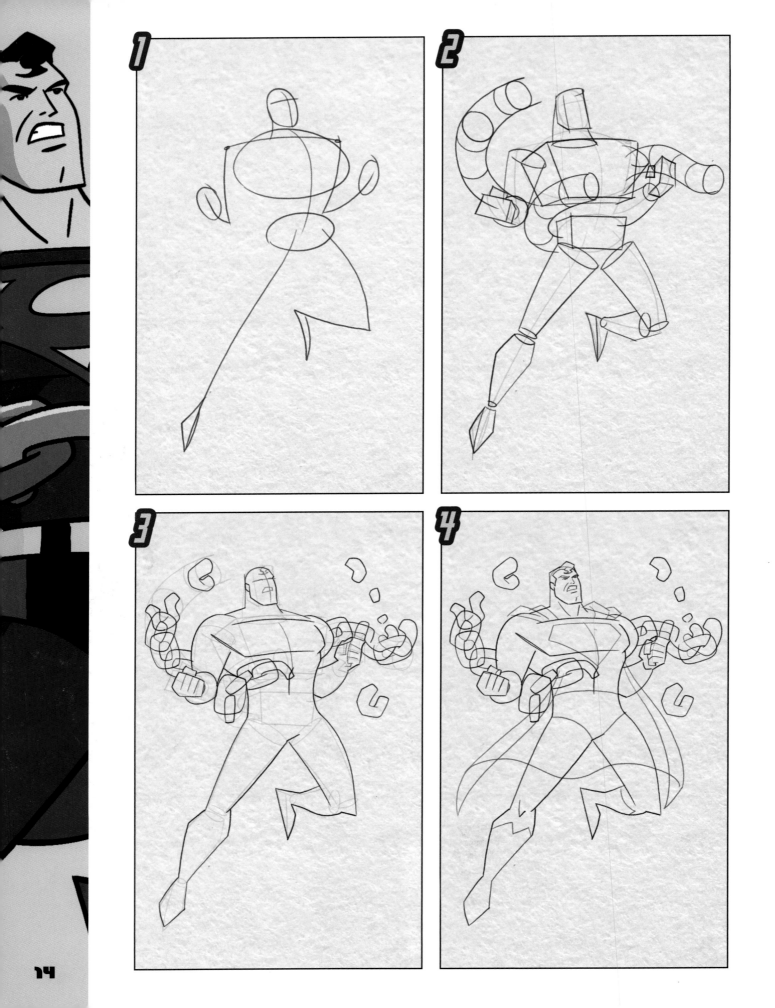

SUPER-STRENGTH

Powered by the sun's yellow light, there is almost no limit to Superman's strength. Even the strongest chains ever created would be no match for his mighty muscles. However, the Man of Steel is powerless against Kryptonite. This radioactive material robs him of his super-strength and other powers. Superman's powers are also useless against magical attacks.

DRAWING IDEA

Now try drawing the Man of Steel picking up a plane, train, or other heavy vehicle!

HEAT VISION

Heat vision is one of Superman's most powerful and useful abilities. He can use it to smash rocks or blast through concrete walls. Superman can also focus this power and use it like a laser beam. He often uses this ability to cut through steel plates or weld objects together to save people in danger.

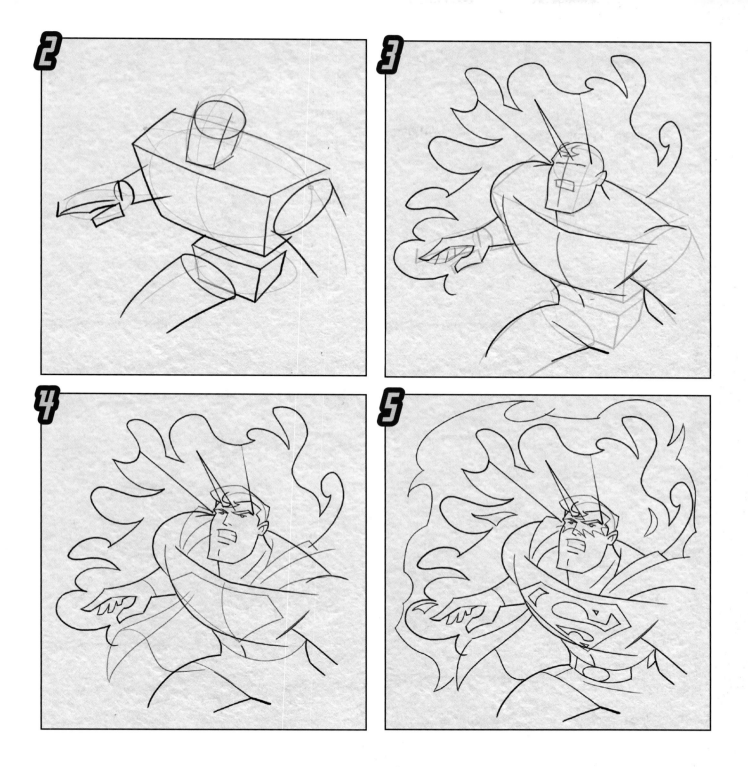

SUPER-BREATH

Superman also has superpowered lungs! When needed, he can blow a powerful blast of air with the force of a hurricane. Superman can also chill his breath to freeze things in an instant. If a dam breaks, Superman's breath can freeze the water and keep the flood from destroying a nearby city.

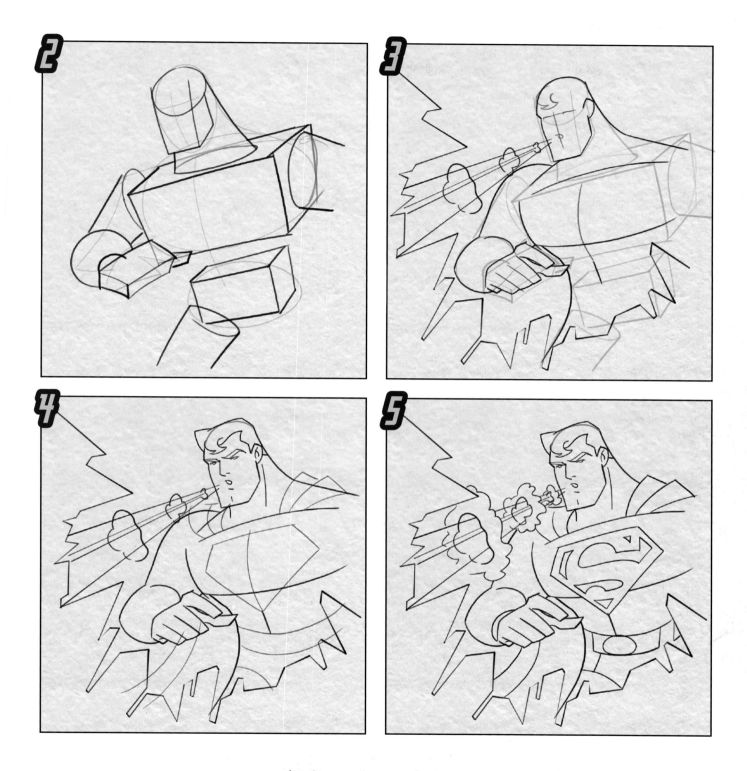

DEFENDING EARTH

Threats to Earth and its people don't always come from villains' evil plans. Superman stays alert for natural disasters and threats from space too. When an asteroid is on course to hit Earth, the Man of Steel is ready. He flies into space to meet it head-on. With one swing of his mighty fist, he can smash the rock to bits and keep it from slamming into the planet.

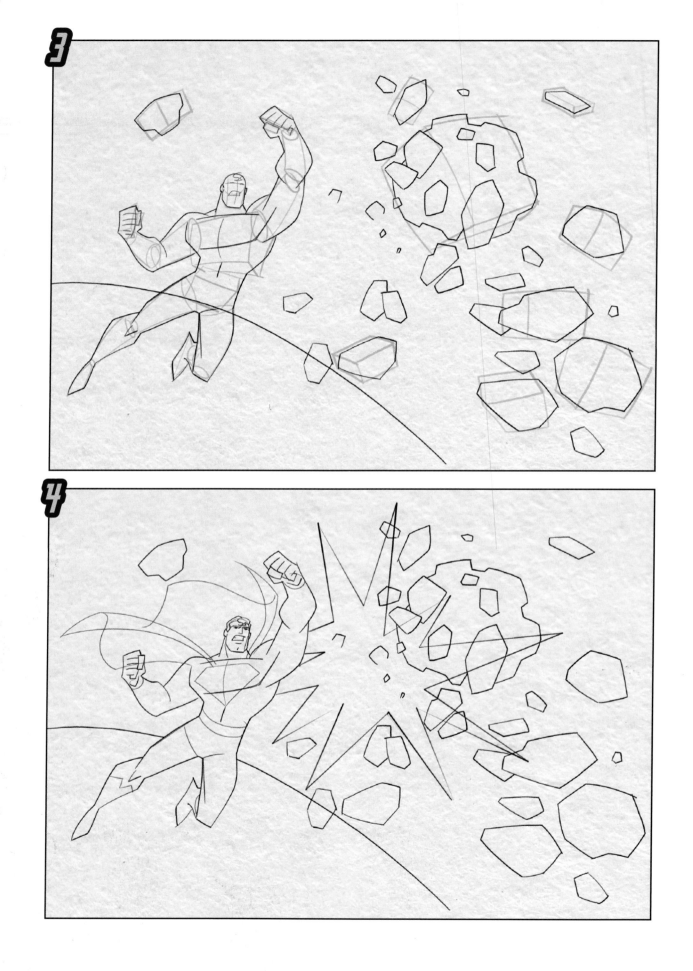

THE KENTS

Name: Jonathan and Martha Kent

Home Base: Smallville, Kansas

Occupation: farmers

Abilities: none

Background: The Kents had no children of their own. When they found young Kal-El and his spaceship near their farm, they adopted the boy and named him Clark. The Kents raised Clark to have strong moral values. They taught him to always do the right thing and to help people whenever possible. Clark is close to his parents and visits them whenever he can.

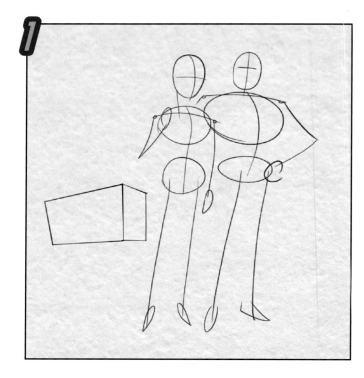

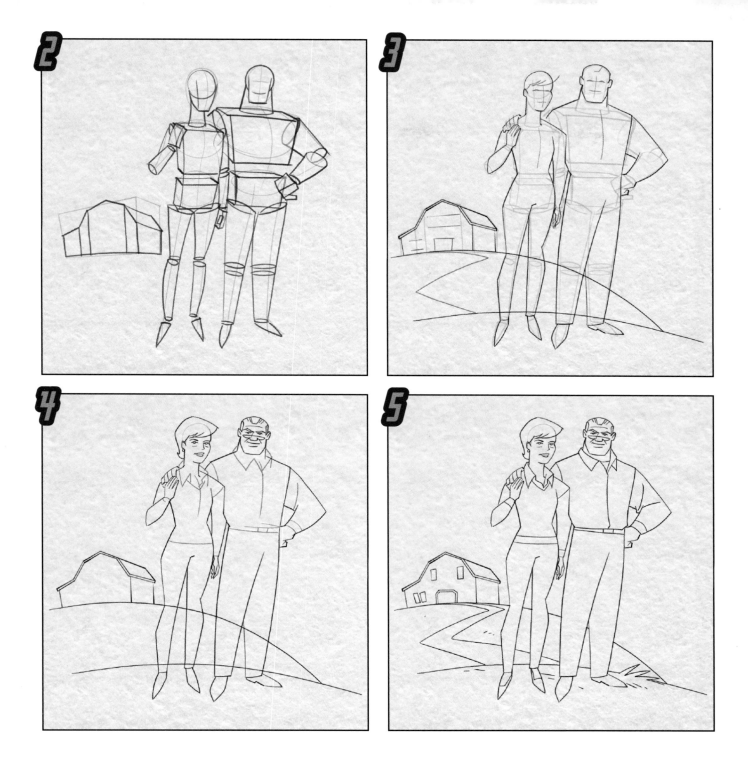

DRAWING IDEA
Next try drawing Clark using his powers to help do chores on the family farm.

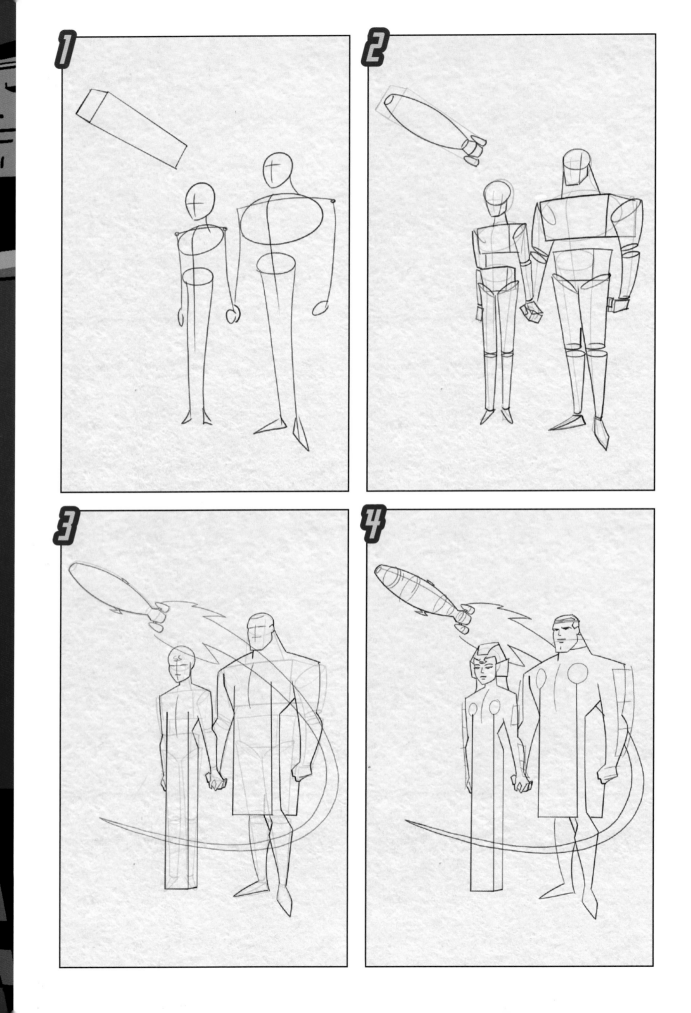

THE FAMILY OF EL

Name: Jor-El and Lara-El

Home Base: Krypton

Occupation: scientists

Abilities: scientific genius

DRAWING IDEA
Now try drawing Superman's home planet. What do you think Krypton looks like?

Background: Jor-El was a scientist on Krypton who predicted the planet's destruction. Unfortunately, Krypton's rulers didn't believe him. But his predictions were soon proven correct when violent quakes began tearing the planet apart. Shortly before Krypton's final destruction, Jor-El and Lara sent their baby son Kal-El to Earth in an experimental spacecraft.

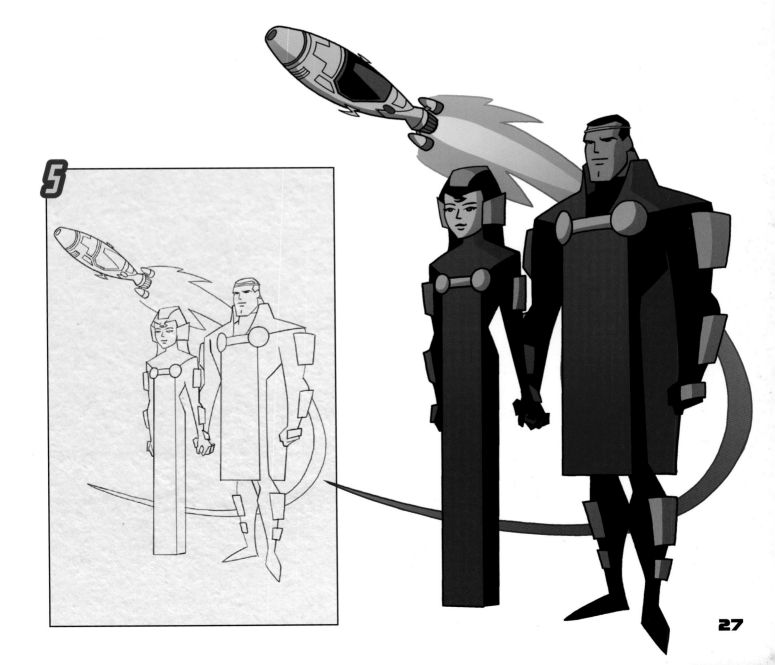

DAILY PLANET FRIENDS

Names: Lois Lane and Jimmy Olsen

Home Base: Daily Planet Building, Metropolis

Occupation: reporter; photographer

Abilities: strong investigation skills

Background: Everybody needs a few good friends, including the Man of Steel. Clark's closest friends work with him at the *Daily Planet.* Jimmy is a photographer and often gets the best photos of Superman. Lois works closely with Clark to cover the biggest news stories in Metropolis.

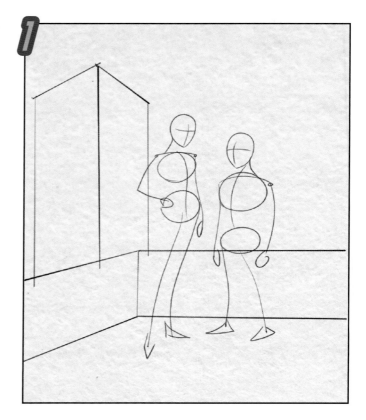

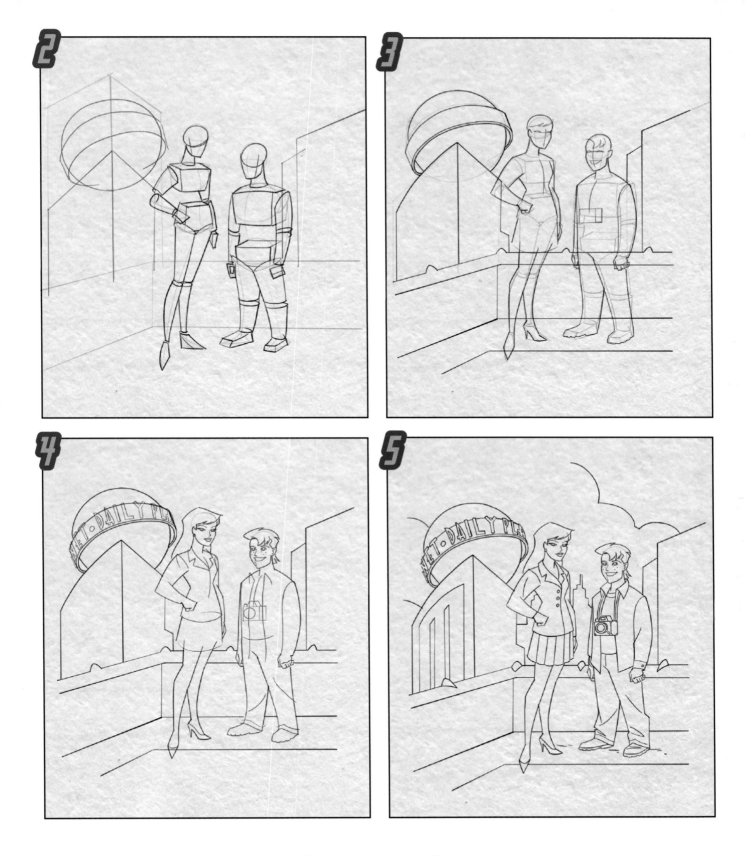

DRAWING IDEA

Now try drawing Clark, Lois, and Jimmy covering a major story in downtown Metropolis.

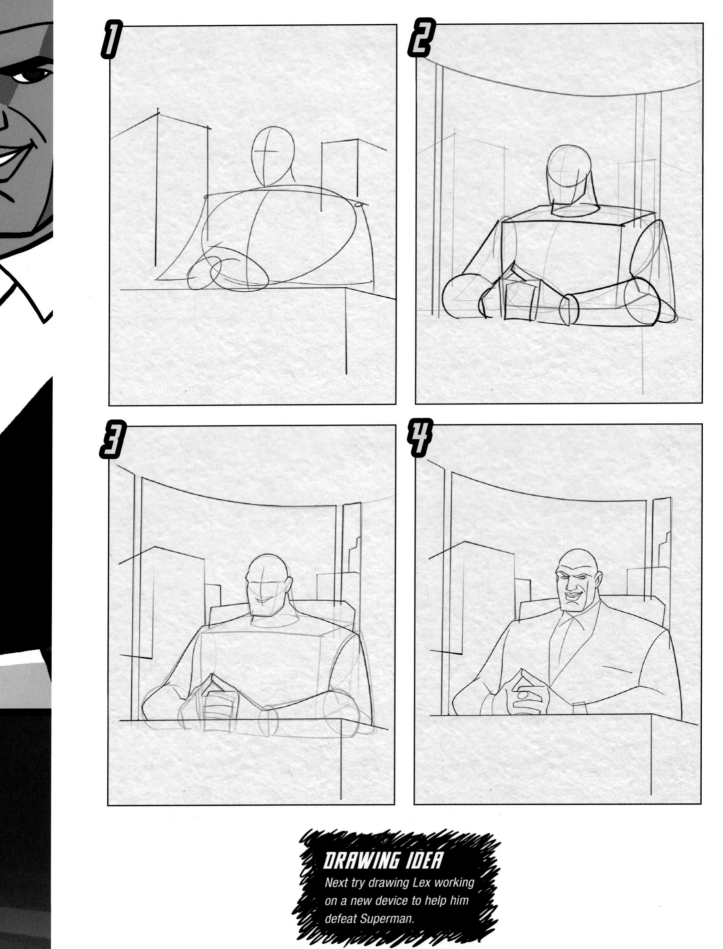

DRAWING IDEA

Next try drawing Lex working on a new device to help him defeat Superman.

LEX LUTHOR

Real Name: Alexander "Lex" Luthor

Home Base: LexCorp, Metropolis

Occupation: successful businessman, criminal mastermind

Enemy of: Superman

Abilities: scientific genius

Background: Lex Luthor is one of the richest and most powerful people in Metropolis. But Superman knows Lex's dirty secret—that he gained most of his wealth through crime. Lex is always careful not to get caught breaking the law red-handed. Lex doesn't have superpowers. However, he has invented several amazing electronic devices to help him succeed in his criminal activities.

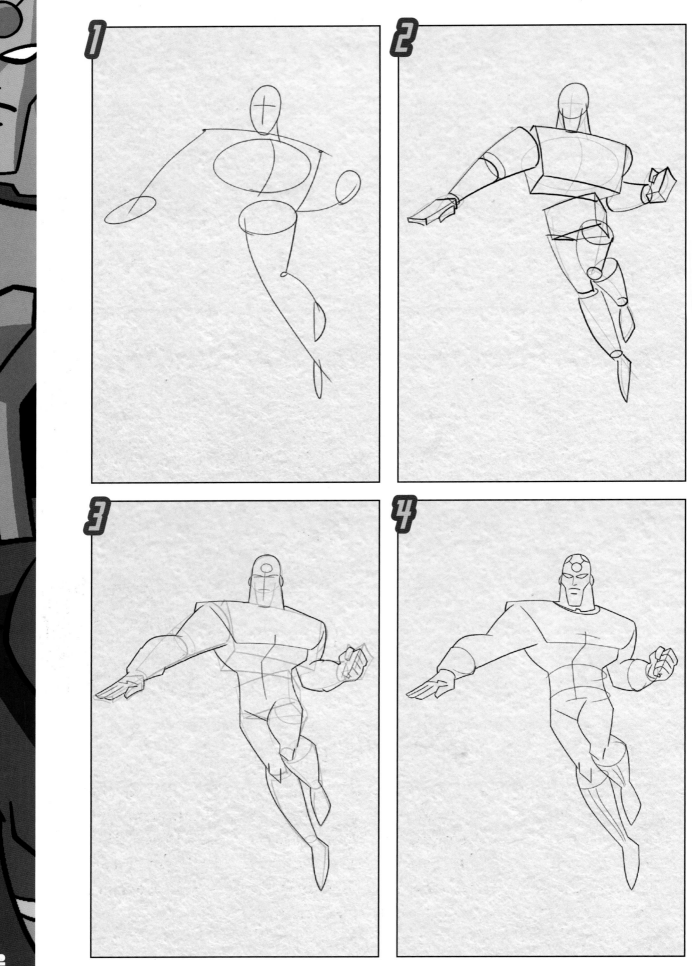

BRAINIAC

Real Name: unknown

Home Base: Skull Ship

Occupation: super-villain

Enemy of: Superman

Abilities: genius intelligence, enhanced strength, flight, master of technology

Background: Brainiac was once a powerful computer on Krypton. It became so intelligent that it became self-aware and left the planet before it was destroyed. Now Brainiac travels the universe, destroying countless planets to harvest their technologies. Brainiac can take control of most forms of technology and uses its vast knowledge to outsmart anyone who stands in its way. Only Superman can match the wits and strength of the walking, talking computer.

DRAWING IDEA

Next try drawing Brainiac's powerful skull-shaped spaceship!

DOOMSDAY

Real Name: Doomsday

Home Base: Krypton

Occupation: destroyer

Enemy of: Superman

Abilities: super-strength and speed, regeneration, invincibility

DRAWING IDEA
After drawing Doomsday, try drawing him in a major battle with the Man of Steel!

Background: Doomsday is an indestructible force of rage. He desires only to destroy everything in his path. The creature is nearly impossible to stop. If he dies, he just comes back to life stronger than before—and is also immune to whatever killed him! Doomsday's body is covered with sharp, jagged bones that he uses as both armor and dangerous weapons. His superpowers and violent nature make Doomsday one of the Man of Steel's deadliest foes.

1

DRAWING IDEA
Next try drawing Parasite
using his powers to steal
Superman's strength!

PARASITE

Real Name: Rudy Jones

Home Base: Metropolis

Occupation: professional criminal and super-villain

Abilities: absorbs energy, powers, and knowledge of others

Background: One night Rudy Jones was trying to steal special chemicals
from a Metropolis laboratory. But as he was fleeing the scene, he was
accidentally soaked in the toxic liquids. The chemicals transformed him
into the monstrous Parasite. Now he can absorb the energy and abilities of
others—especially the mighty powers of the Man of Steel.

BIZARRO

Real Name: unknown

Home Base: Bizarro World

Occupation: super-villain

Enemy of: Superman

Abilities: super-strength, flight, freeze vision, fire breath

Background: Bizarro is a twisted clone of Superman created by Lex Luthor. Bizarro's powers are equal yet opposite to Superman's. For example, instead of fiery heat vision, Bizarro blasts beams of ice from his eyes. He is also unpredictable and doesn't know his own strength, making him a dangerous threat to Metropolis.

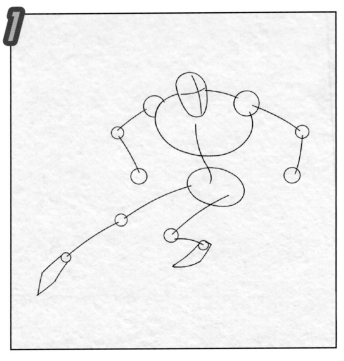

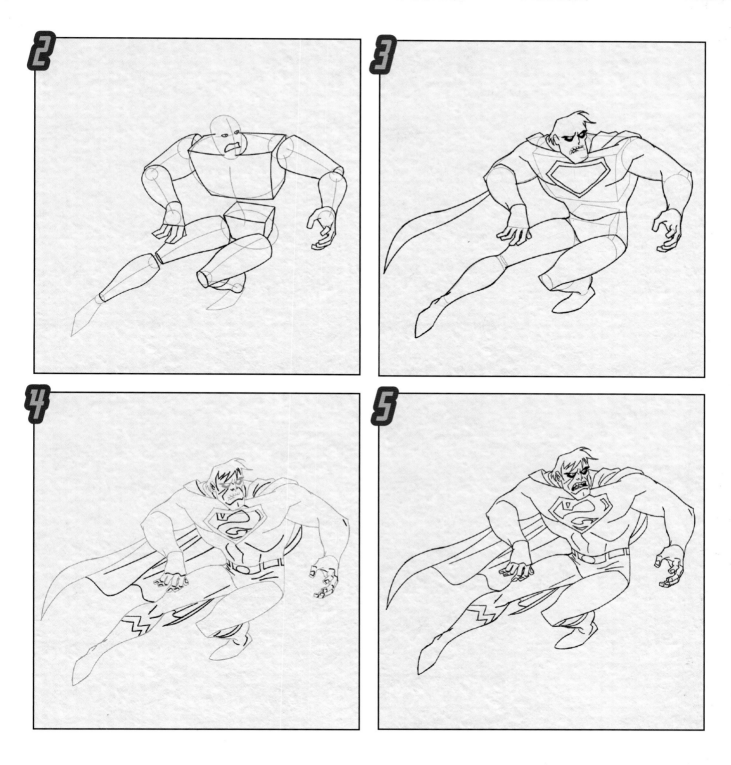

METALLO

Real Name: John Corben

Home Base: Metropolis

Occupation: criminal and super-villain

Enemy of: Superman

Abilities: enhanced strength and speed, metal transformation

Background: John Corben was a criminal once employed by Lex Luthor. While in prison, Luthor infected Corben with a deadly disease. To save himself, Corben agreed to an experimental medical procedure. But when he woke, he discovered that his brain had been placed into a cyborg body powered by green Kryptonite. Now known as Metallo, he is nearly as strong and fast as Superman. The radiation from his Kryptonite heart can be lethal for the Man of Steel.

DRAWING IDEA

Try drawing Metallo using his Kryptonite powers in a face-off against the Man of Steel!

GENERAL ZOD

Real Name: Dru-Zod

Home Base: Krypton

Occupation: criminal warlord

Enemy of: Superman

Abilities: super-strength, speed, and breath; heat vision; flight; invincibility

Background: General Zod was a military leader who tried to take over Krypton, but failed. As punishment Zod and his followers were banished to the mysterious Phantom Zone. When they escaped, Zod decided that he would rule over Earth instead of Krypton. Luckily Superman is there to stop Zod and his evil plans. However, Zod's powers match those of Superman. Defeating this warrior from Krypton will be the Man of Steel's greatest challenge.

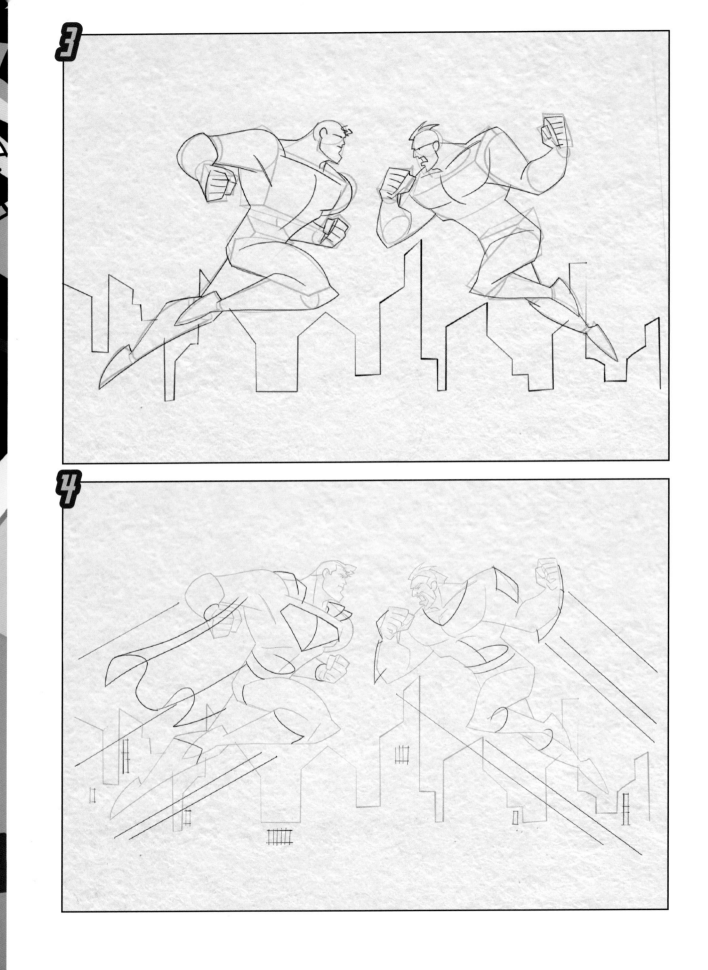

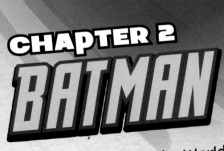

CHAPTER 2
BATMAN

He's been called the World's Greatest Detective, the Caped Crusader, and the Dark Knight. But whatever people choose to call him—Batman is a criminal's worst nightmare.

As a young boy, Bruce Wayne lost his parents, Thomas and Martha, during a robbery in a dark alley. Bruce took his parents' death very hard. He swore an oath that he would do whatever it took to rid Gotham City of criminals and crime. To achieve his goal, Bruce studied criminology to learn detective skills. He also trained hard to become an expert in martial arts. He even became a master of disguise and an expert escape artist.

Bruce's new skills were useful, but they weren't enough for him. He also wanted to strike fear into the hearts of lawbreakers. Bruce chose to use his own fear of bats as inspiration. He made a special suit resembling a giant bat to hide his identity and to frighten hardened criminals. With his Batsuit and unmatched crime-fighting skills, Bruce became Batman, the Dark Knight! Welcome to the world of Batman! Are you ready to begin drawing Batman, his friends, and several of his most infamous enemies?

Imagine the streets of Gotham City and see what kind of amazing Batman drawings you can create!

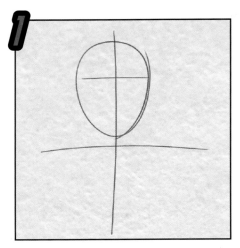

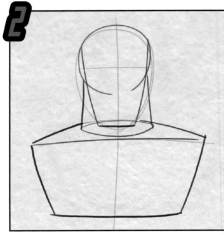

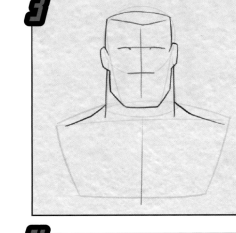

BRUCE WAYNE

Most people in Gotham City know Bruce Wayne as the billionaire owner of Wayne Enterprises. He gives generously to charities to help Gotham City and its citizens. However, Bruce's public behavior is all an act to hide his secret identity as the Dark Knight.

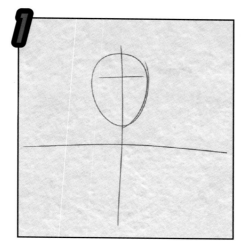

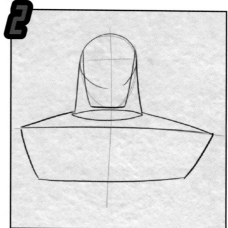

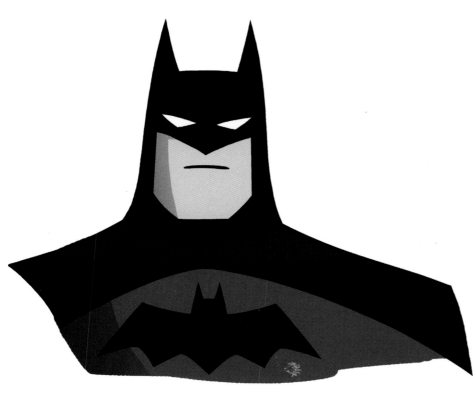

BATMAN

At night Bruce prowls the streets of Gotham as Batman. When he sees a crime taking place, he's ready to swing into action. Batman uses his fine-tuned fighting skills and incredible gadgets to stop criminals in their tracks. He usually leaves crooks tied up at the scene of the crime for the police to pick up later.

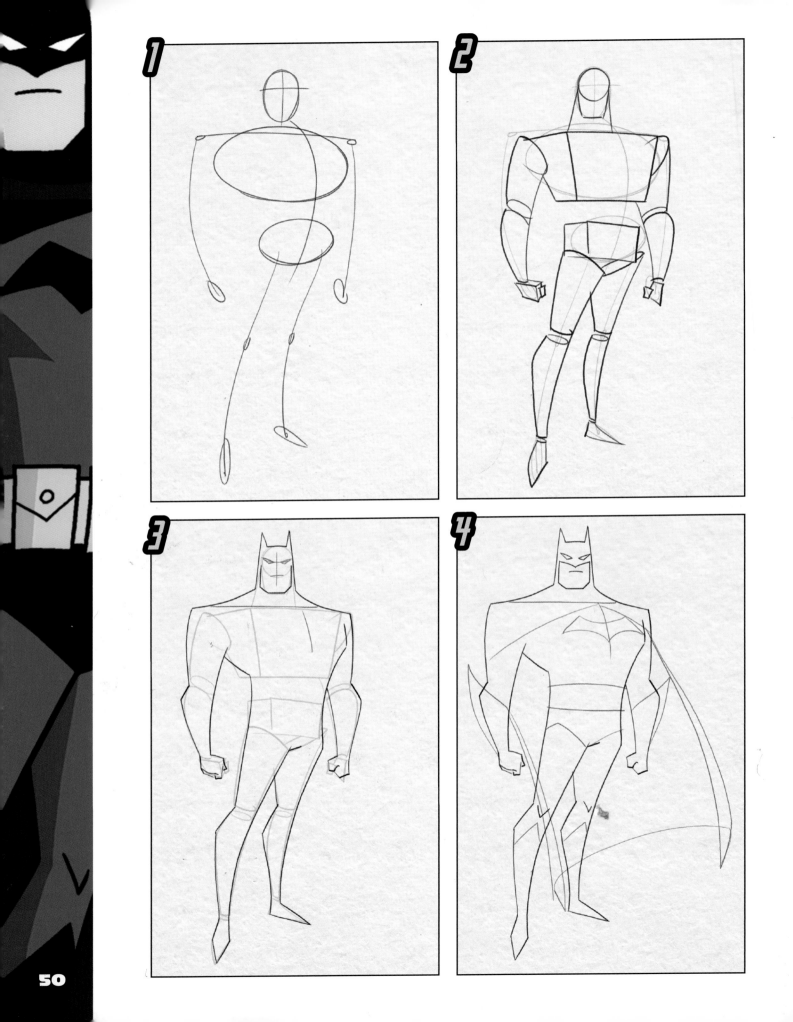

BATSUIT

Batman wouldn't be Batman without his Batsuit. The suit's main purpose is to hide Bruce Wayne's identity while striking terror in the hearts of criminals. The suit also helps Batman hide in the shadows as he prowls through the night. Batman's Utility Belt holds his many crime-fighting tools, including batarangs, a grapnel, binoculars, and remote controls for his vehicles.

BATCAVE

Sometimes the World's Greatest Detective needs a quiet place to think. When Batman needs answers, he heads to his secret Batcave. There he uses the powerful Batcomputer to study clues and learn the information he needs. The Batcave is also home to Batman's amazing vehicles and his workshop where he creates his incredible crime-fighting gadgets.

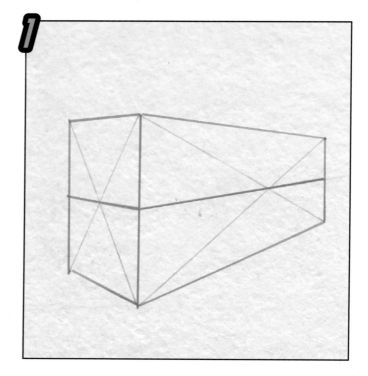

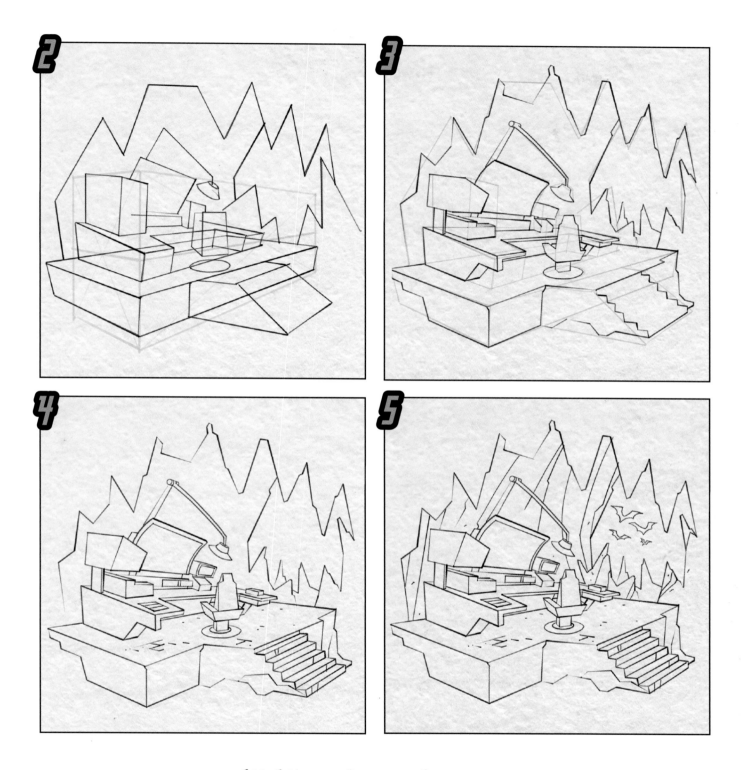

DRAWING IDEA
Next try drawing the Batmobile blasting out of the Batcave's secret entrance!

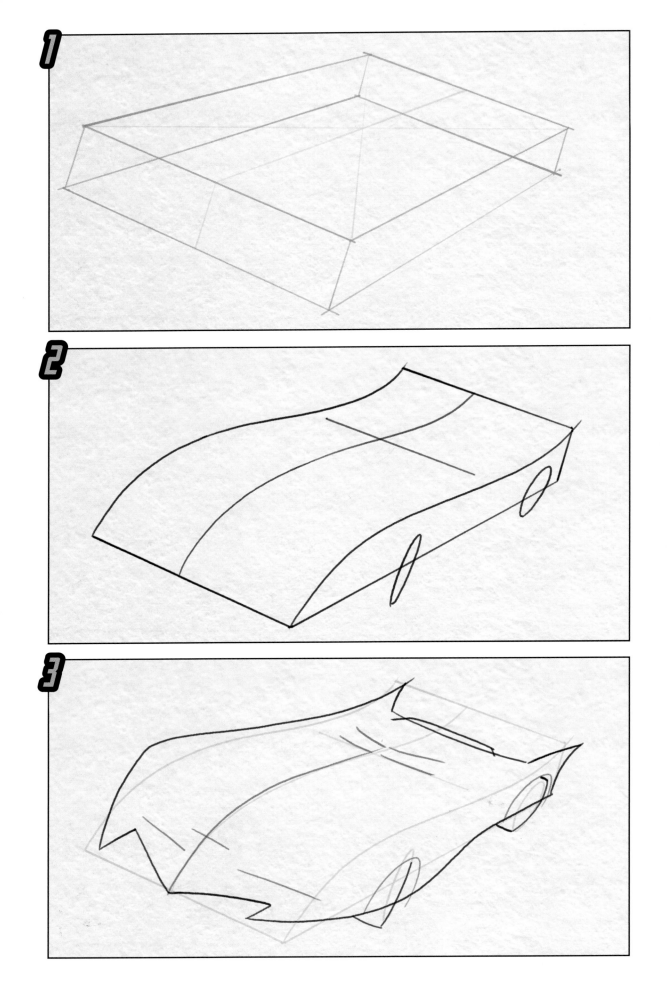

BATMOBILE

When Batman needs to get somewhere fast, he relies on the Batmobile to get him there. With its jet-powered engine, this speedy car helps Batman travel across Gotham City in a flash. Batman also uses the Batmobile to chase down villains in their getaway cars. The armored car is equipped with grappling hooks and road spikes. It can also create slippery oil slicks to stop criminals from escaping.

DRAWING IDEA
Try drawing the Batmobile chasing Two-Face's getaway car after a bank robbery!

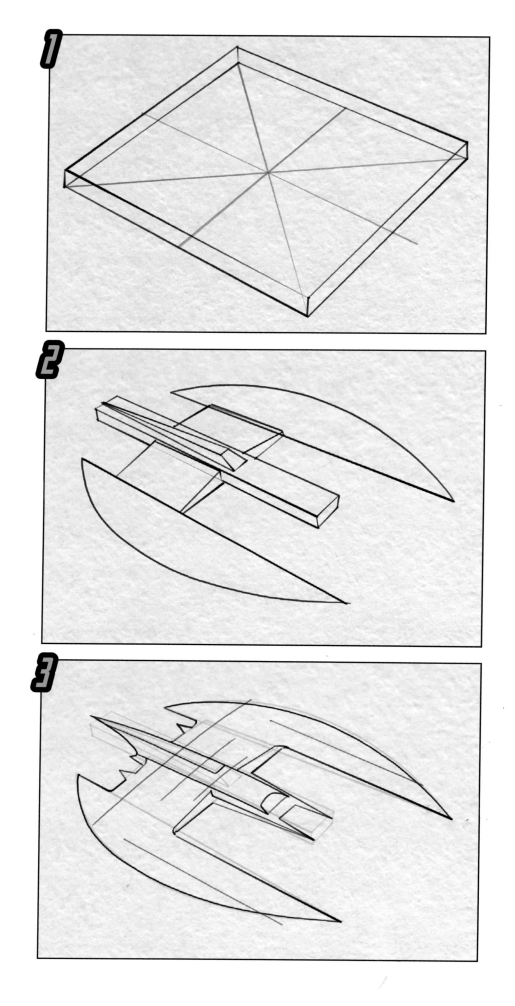

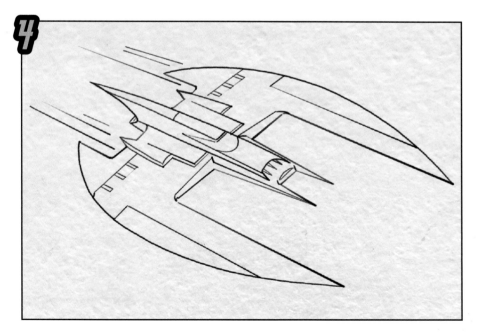

BATWING

Sometimes Batman's crime-fighting work requires him to take to the sky. The Batwing can fly at incredible speeds to block deadly threats from the air. It can also hover in place to ambush enemies from above. The Batwing is equipped with a front grappling arm and claw. The claw can carry heavy objects or grab people in midair and carry them to safety.

DRAWING IDEA
Next try showing the Batwing take out a deadly missile launched by the Joker!

1

2

3

4

BATARANGS

Batman hates guns and refuses to use them. He instead uses special boomerang-like Batarangs to stun enemies and disarm them. Explosive Batarangs are useful for demolishing obstacles. Electric Batarangs can be used to disrupt electronic systems. These weapons are one of Batman's most useful crime-fighting tools.

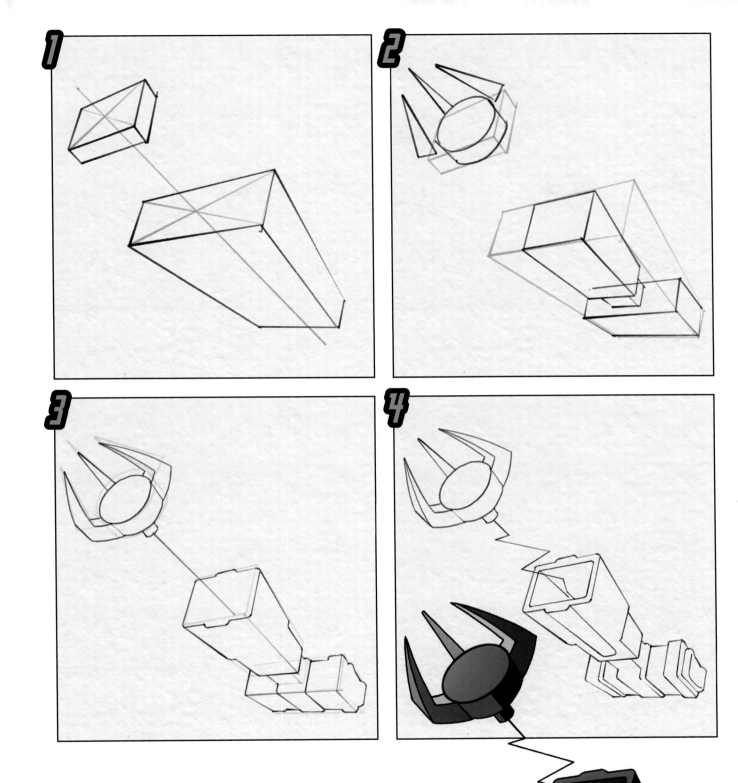

BATMAN'S GRAPNEL

Batman relies on his powerful grapnel to reach Gotham City's rooftops. This handy device shoots out a strong claw that can grab and hold onto nearly any surface. The attached cable then pulls Batman up to his target. He can also use the grapnel to grab enemies or disarm them, or even to pull down walls.

FIGHTING CRIME

Criminals in Gotham City don't stand a chance with Batman around. He's always on the lookout for thugs trying to break the law. When a super-villain like Bane tries to rob a bank, the Dark Knight is on the case. Bane is very intelligent and has superhuman strength. But Batman's fighting skills and experience can stop the master criminal in his tracks!

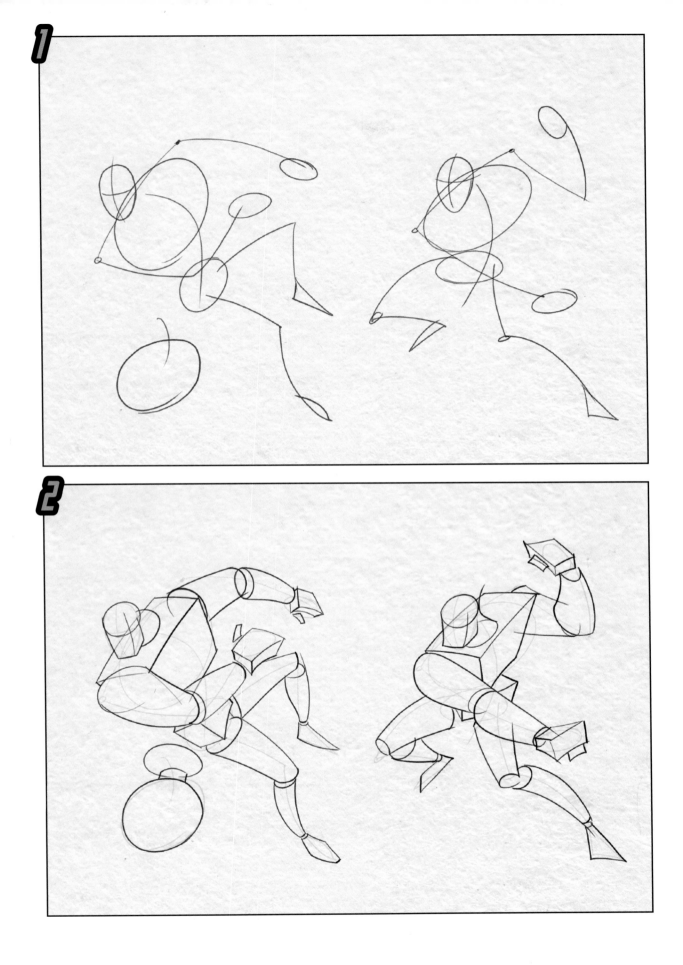

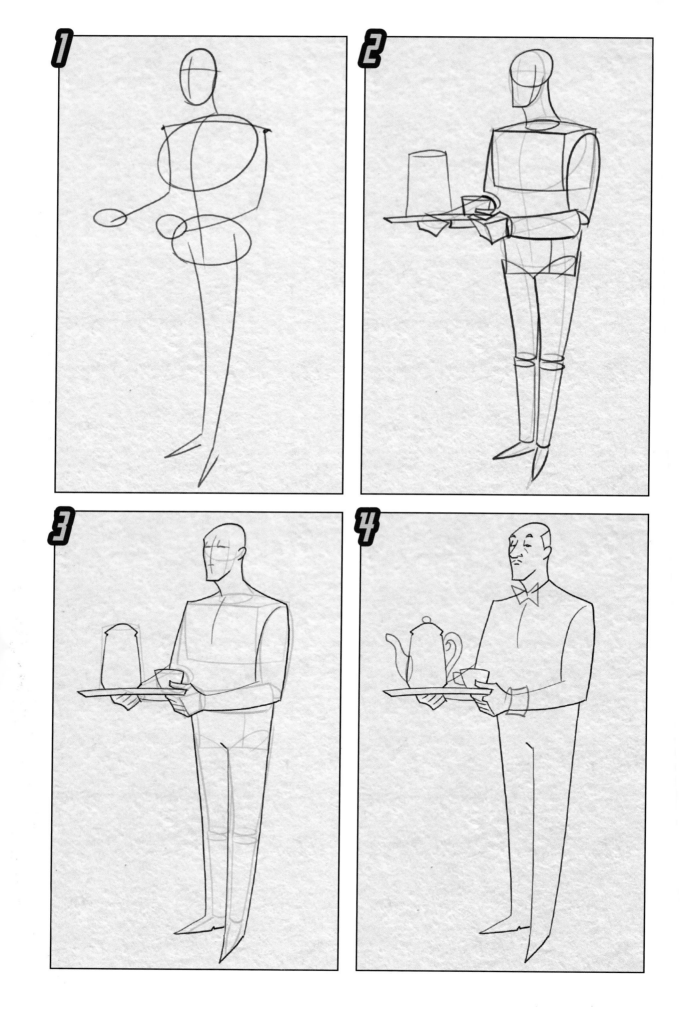

DRAWING IDEA
Try drawing Alfred helping Batman repair the Batmobile in the Batcave.

ALFRED

Name: Alfred Pennyworth

Home Base: Wayne Manor, Gotham City

Occupation: butler

Abilities: cooking, housekeeping, computer operation, investigation, spying skills

Background: Alfred Pennyworth was the butler to the Wayne family. When Bruce Wayne's parents died, Alfred became like a father to Bruce. He took care of Bruce and provided him with guidance and moral support as he grew up. Alfred is fiercely loyal and fully supports Bruce's mission as Batman. As a skilled mechanic, medic, and spy, Alfred is the Dark Knight's closest friend and most valued assistant.

1

DRAWING IDEA
After drawing Robin, try drawing him fighting next to Batman to put a stop to the Riddler's plans!

ROBIN, THE BOY WONDER

Real Name: Tim Drake

Home Base: Gotham City

Occupation: student, crime fighter

Abilities: martial arts expert, investigation skills

Background: Tim Drake is quite brilliant for his age. Using his keen observation skills, Tim learned the secret identities of both Batman and Nightwing. Nightwing had once fought crime next to Batman as the first Robin. Nightwing then helped Tim convince Batman that he needed a new partner. Tim now fights crime alongside Batman as the all new Robin, the Boy Wonder.

5

DRAWING IDEA
Try drawing Batgirl working with Robin to track down the Penguin and his thugs!

BATGIRL

Real Name: Barbara Gordon

Home Base: Gotham City

Occupation: college student, crime fighter

Abilities: gymnastics, martial arts skills

Background: Barbara Gordon takes after her father, Police Commissioner James Gordon. She is strong-willed and dedicated to wiping out crime in Gotham City. When Barbara's father was framed for a crime he didn't commit, she made her own bat-themed suit and attempted to break him out of jail. Since then Batgirl has become part of Batman's team, helping him defend Gotham City from crime.

COMMISSIONER GORDON

Name: James "Jim" Gordon

Home Base: Gotham City

Occupation: police commissioner

Abilities: police work, investigative skills

Background: Jim Gordon is Gotham City's Head of Police. At first he didn't approve of Batman's methods. He felt that Batman was getting in the way of police business. But Gordon soon realized that Batman was fighting for justice. Now when he needs help or has important information to share, he lights up the Bat-Signal to get the Dark Knight's attention. Gordon and Batman work closely together to take down Gotham City's worst criminals.

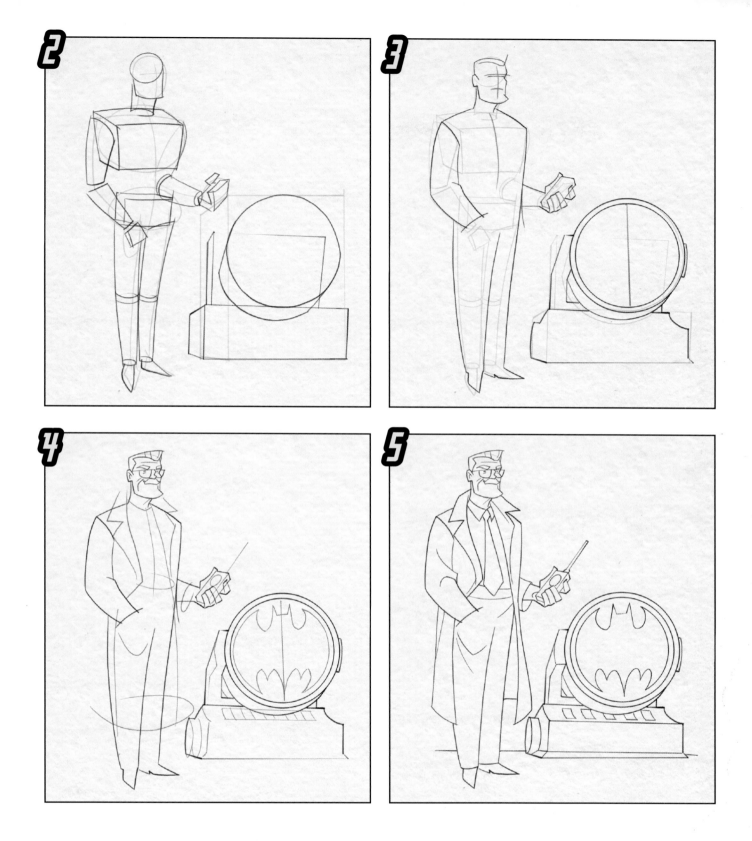

THE JOKER

Real Name: unknown

Home Base: Gotham City

Occupation: professional criminal

Enemy of: Batman

Abilities: above-average strength, genius-level intelligence, skills in chemistry and engineering

Background: Also known as the Clown Prince of Crime, the Joker is Batman's most dangerous enemy. When he fell into a vat of toxic waste, he was transformed into an evil madman. The chemicals bleached his skin white, dyed his hair green, and peeled his lips back into a permanent, hideous grin. The Joker delights in tormenting Batman and the innocent people of Gotham City.

DRAWING IDEA
Try drawing the Joker with a deadly hand buzzer or other practical joke device.

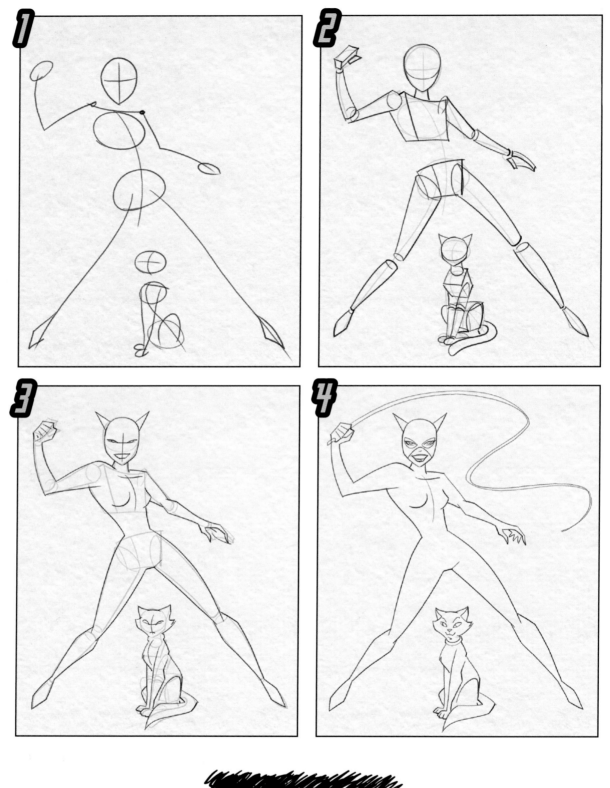

DRAWING IDEA

Next try drawing Catwoman working with Batman to stop Mr. Freeze's wicked plans!

CATWOMAN

Real Name: Selina Kyle

Home Base: Gotham City

Occupation: professional thief

Abilities: stealth, gymnastics, and martial arts skills

Equipment: retractable claws

Background: Selina Kyle became an orphan at a young age. She grew up committing petty crimes to survive on the streets. Now as Catwoman, Selina is an incredibly stealthy and skilled burglar. She preys on Gotham City's wealthy citizens while protecting the city's less fortunate people. Selina has helped Batman stop major criminals on several occasions. But their partnerships never last long. She has no interest in ending her own thieving ways.

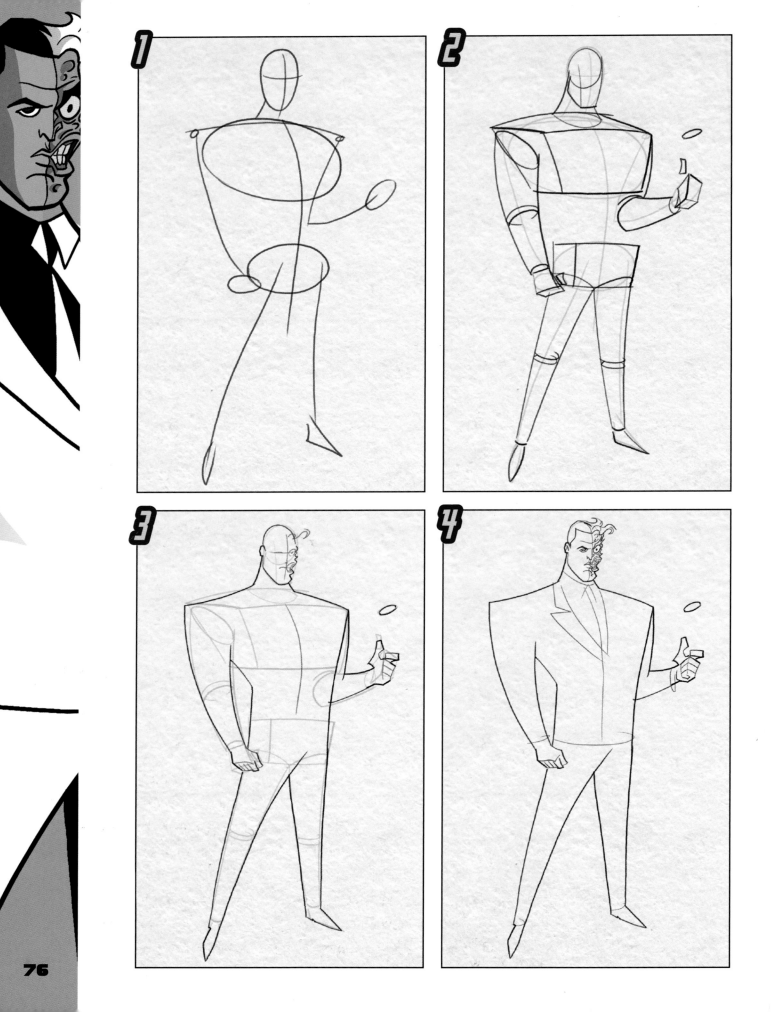

TWO-FACE

Real Name: Harvey Dent
Home Base: Gotham City
Occupation: professional criminal
Enemy of: Batman
Abilities: above-average strength and fighting skills, expert marksmanship
Equipment: special two-headed coin to make most decisions

Background: Harvey Dent was once the best prosecuting attorney in Gotham City. He worked tirelessly to send the city's most dangerous criminals to jail. But when an explosion scarred half of his face and body, Harvey's darker side took control. He became the criminal Two-Face. Now he tries to run the same criminal world he once fought so hard to bring to justice.

DRAWING IDEA
After drawing Two-Face, show him in a fight against Batman after robbing an armored car.

THE RIDDLER

Real Name: Edward Nygma

Home Base: Gotham City

Occupation: professional criminal

Enemy of: Batman

Abilities: genius-level intellect

Equipment: question mark cane containing hidden weapons and gadgets

Background: Edward Nygma loved riddles and puzzles as a boy. When he grew up he invented a popular video game called *Riddle of the Minotaur.* The game sold millions of copies, but Nygma never got a penny for his work. To get his revenge, he became the genius criminal the Riddler. He enjoys leaving cryptic clues to his crimes. Only Batman can solve the Riddler's puzzling crimes and put a stop to his wicked plans.

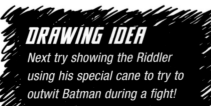

DRAWING IDEA
Next try showing the Riddler using his special cane to try to outwit Batman during a fight!

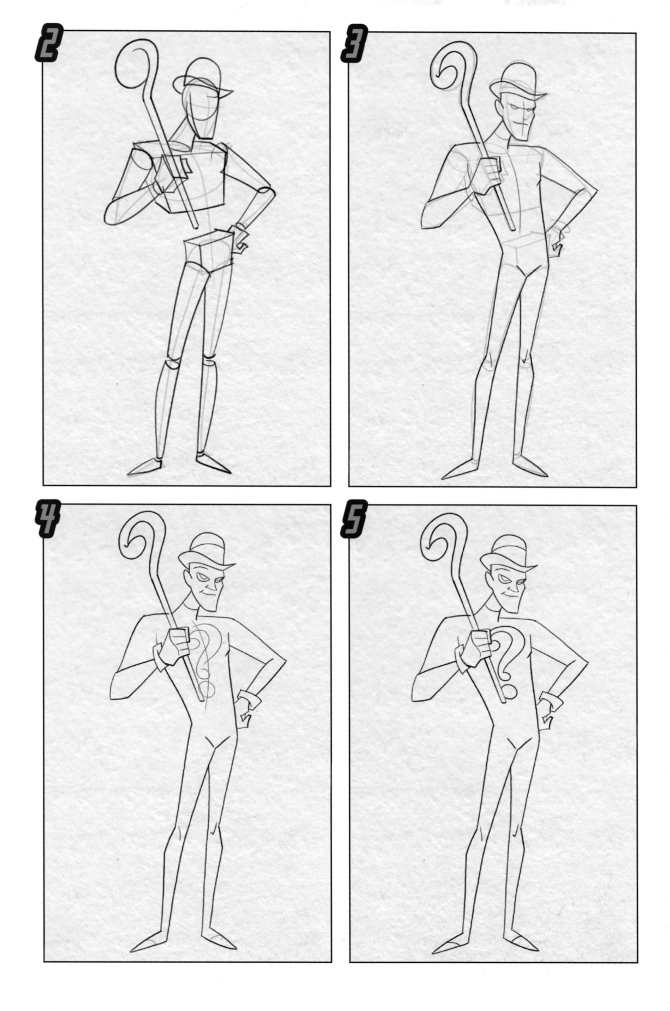

BANE

Real Name: unknown

Home Base: Gotham City

Occupation: assassin and professional criminal

Enemy of: Batman

Abilities: superhuman strength, genius-level intellect

Equipment: Venom drug

Background: Bane's background is a mystery, even to Batman. The only thing known for sure is that Bane was once a prisoner. He was chosen as a test subject for a new drug called Venom. The drug gave Bane superhuman strength. He now uses it to stay strong and works as one of Gotham City's criminal masterminds. Bane's greatest desire is to be the one person who can defeat the Dark Knight—permanently.

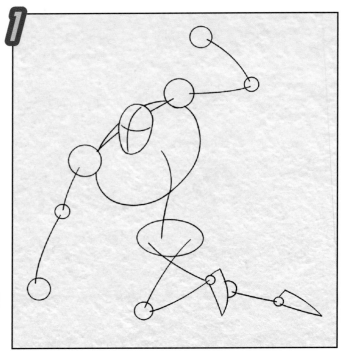

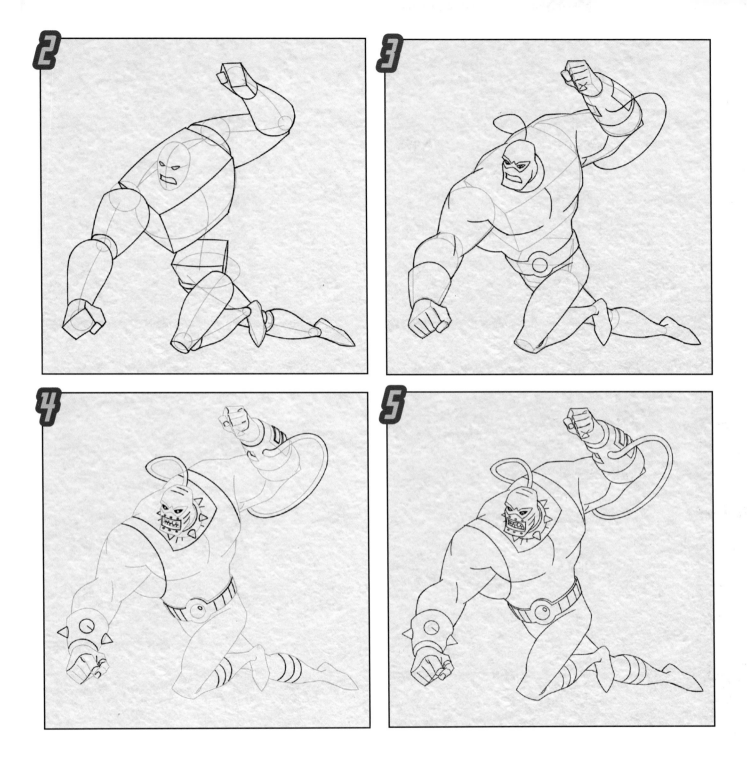

DRAWING IDEA
Try drawing Bane brawling with
Batman on a bridge in Gotham City.

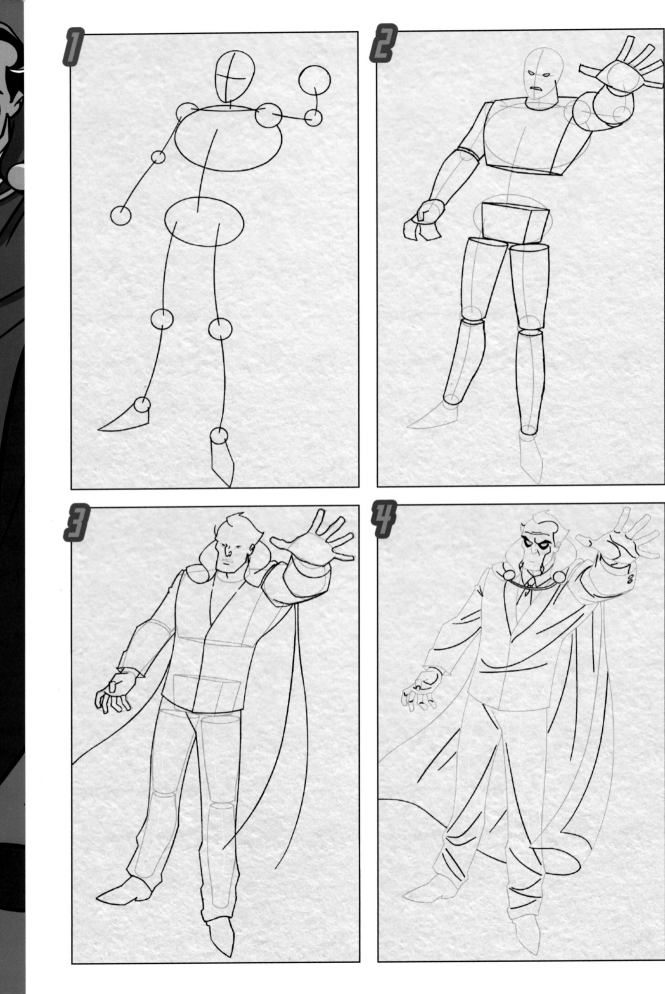

RA'S AL GHUL

Real Name: Ra's al Ghul

Home Base: unknown

Occupation: international ecoterrorist

Abilities: excellent swordsman, genius intellect, near-immortality through use of Lazarus Pits

Background: Ra's al Ghul believes the Earth should be restored to its original unspoiled form. He is completely dedicated to his goals, even if it means wiping out the human race in the process. Ra's has lived for hundreds of years by bathing in Lazarus Pits to maintain his youth and prolong his life. He has gained great wealth and knowledge through his long life. A master of martial arts, Ra's is one of Batman's most dangerous foes.

DRAWING IDEA
Try drawing Ra's al Ghul fighting Batman after restoring his youth in a Lazarus Pit!

STOPPING THE JOKER

The Joker loves being Batman's archenemy. He's always hoping to get the last laugh on the Dark Knight. The Joker enjoys designing weapons with a comical look to hide their true danger. For example, a huge bomb filled with deadly Joker Venom might look like a big party toy. But Batman is very familiar with how the Clown Prince of Crime thinks. He's always ready to swing into action and put a stop to the Joker's plans before innocent people get hurt.

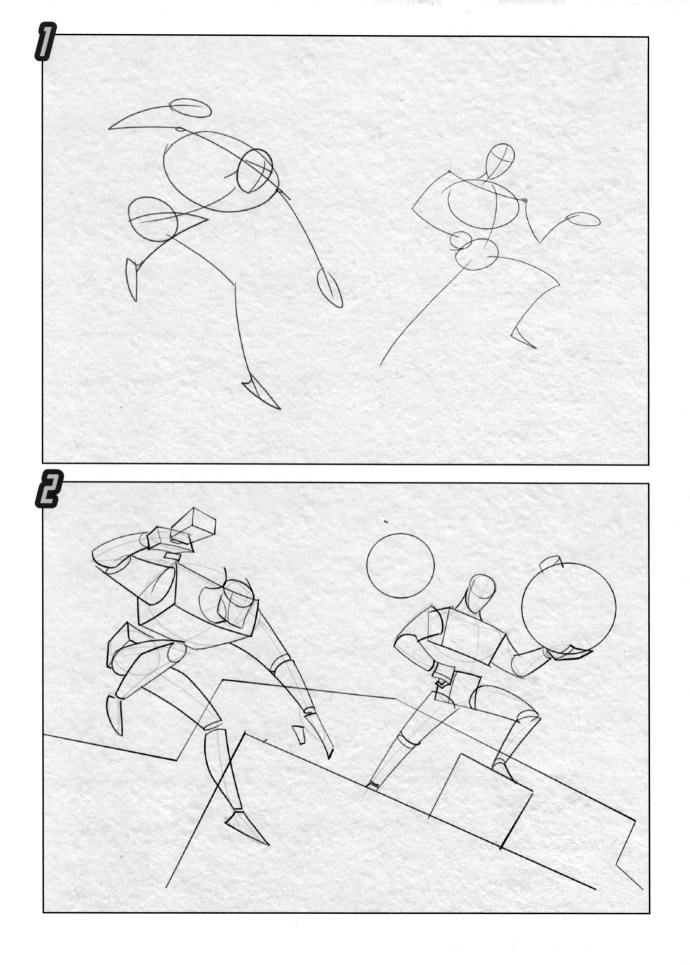

CHAPTER 3
WONDER WOMAN AND OTHER DC SUPER HEROES

Superman and Batman aren't the only super heroes fighting the forces of evil. Wonder Woman, Green Lantern, The Flash, Supergirl, and many other super heroes work just as hard to stop super-villains' wicked plans.

Super heroes come from a wide range of backgrounds and have many different powers. Some are human. Others come from alien worlds. Some heroes grew up with loving families as kids, while others were orphans. Some heroes were born with their abilities. Others got their powers from an accident or received them as gifts. However, as different as they are, super heroes all have one thing in common. They all have a strong desire to fight for justice and protect innocent people.

Welcome to the world of DC Super Heroes! Just turn the page to begin drawing Wonder Woman, Green Lantern, Cyborg, and several other incredible super heroes.

Use the power of your imagination to send your favorite super heroes on new awesome adventures!

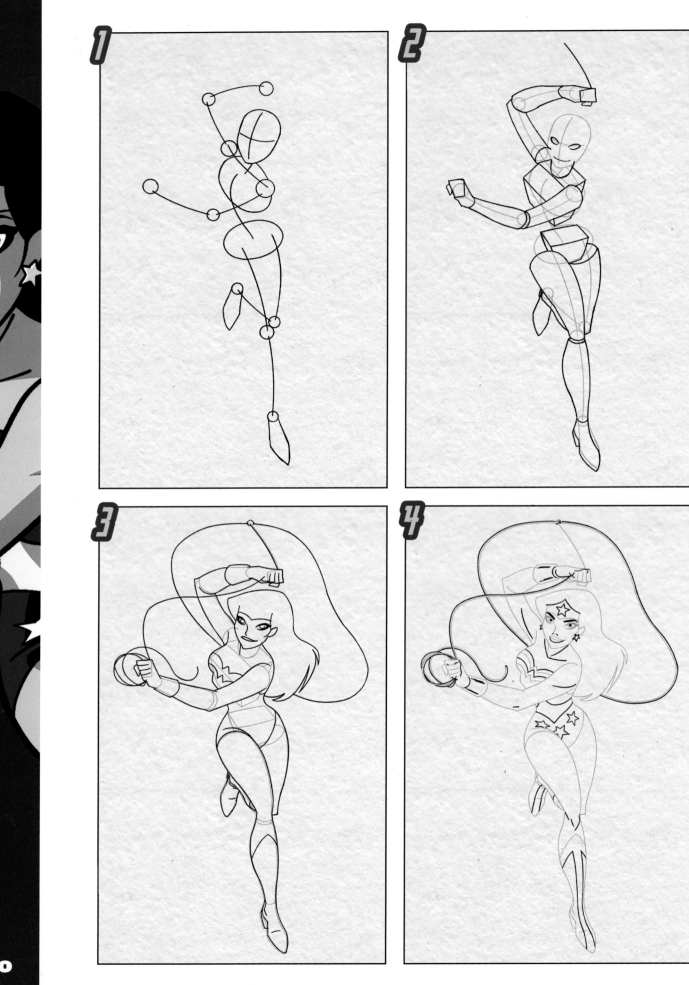

WONDER WOMAN

Real Name: Princess Diana

Home Base: Island of Themyscira

Occupation: Amazon princess, crime fighter

Abilities: super-strength and speed, flight

Equipment: indestructible bracelets, magical tiara, Lasso of Truth

Background: Diana is the Princess of Themyscira, the hidden home of the Amazons. But as she grew up, Diana knew she could be more than just an Amazonian princess. She trained hard and became highly skilled in hand-to-hand combat. Now, with her magical tiara, indestructible bracelets, and Lasso of Truth, Diana fights the forces of evil as Wonder Woman.

GREEN LANTERN

Real Name: Hal Jordan

Home Base: Coast City

Occupation: test pilot, intergalactic police officer

Abilities: green energy weapons and force fields, flight

Equipment: green power ring

Background: Hal Jordan was a brash and reckless test pilot for Ferris Aircraft. One day he discovered the severely injured alien Abin Sur in his crashed spaceship. Before he died Abin Sur gave Hal his Green Lantern power ring. He believed that Hal had the strength of will needed to be part of the Green Lantern Corps. Using the ring's powerful green energy, Hal can create any kind of weapon or force field he can imagine to protect Earth from the forces of evil.

DRAWING IDEA
Next try drawing Green Lantern creating a giant green boxing glove with his ring to knock out the bad guys!

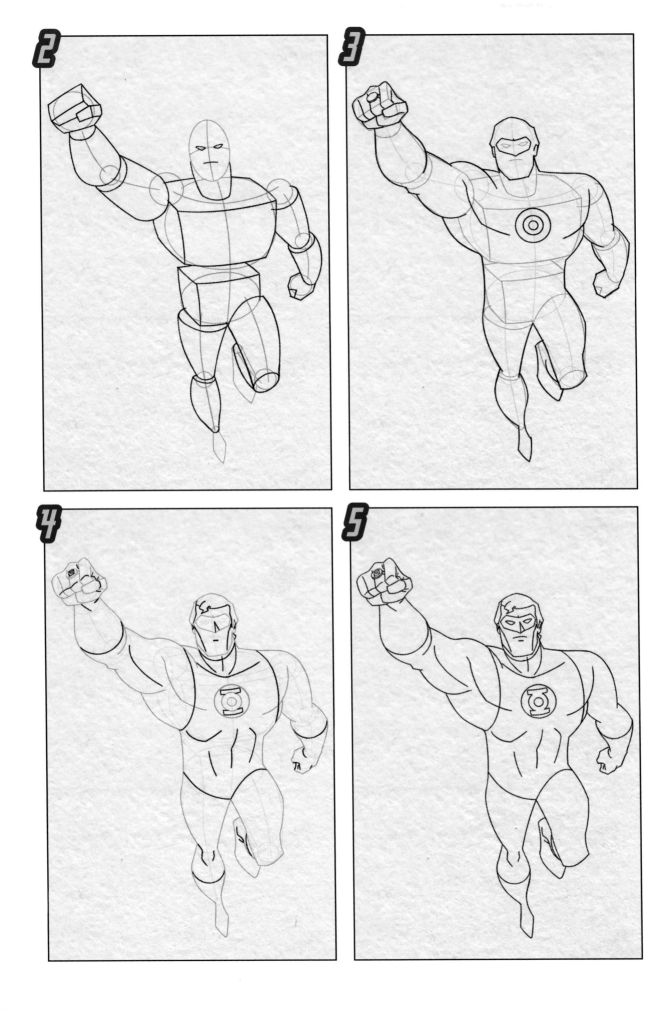

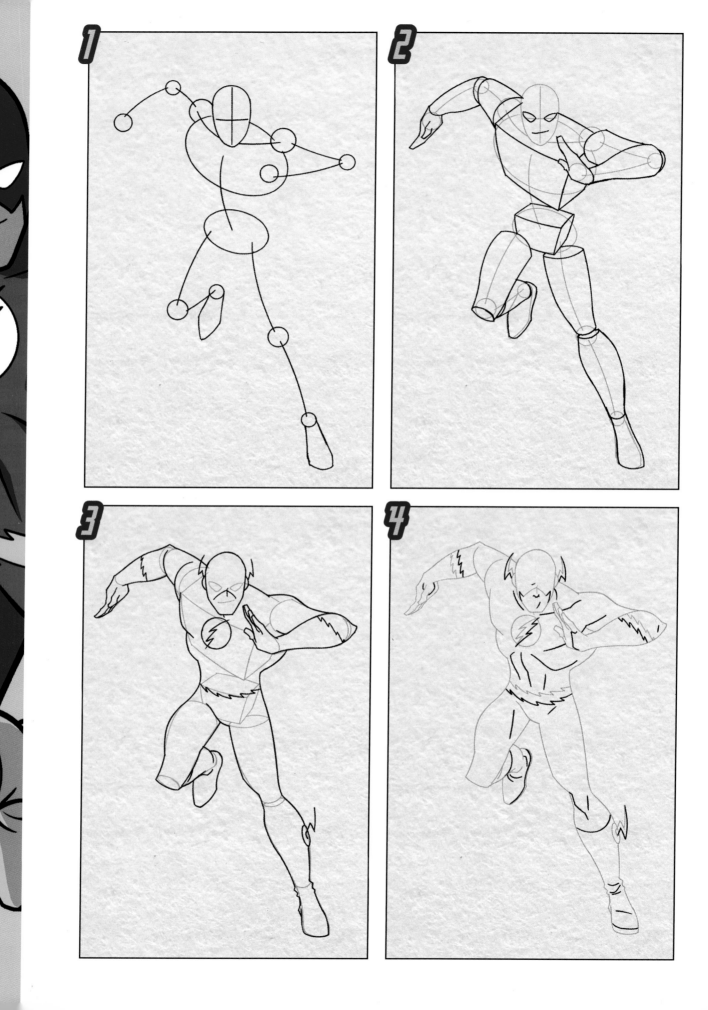

DRAWING IDEA
Try drawing The Flash
outrunning the icy rays
from Captain Cold's gun!

THE FLASH

Real Name: Barry Allen

Home Base: Central City

Occupation: forensic scientist, crime fighter

Abilities: super-speed, accelerated healing, phasing

Background: Forensic scientist Barry Allen was working in his lab one stormy night when a powerful bolt of lightning shot through a window. The lightning destroyed a chemical cabinet, soaking Barry in electrified chemicals. Shortly after the accident Barry discovered he could move at supersonic speeds. He can even vibrate his body so fast that he can phase right through solid walls! As The Flash, Barry uses his super-speed to save people in danger and stop criminals in their tracks.

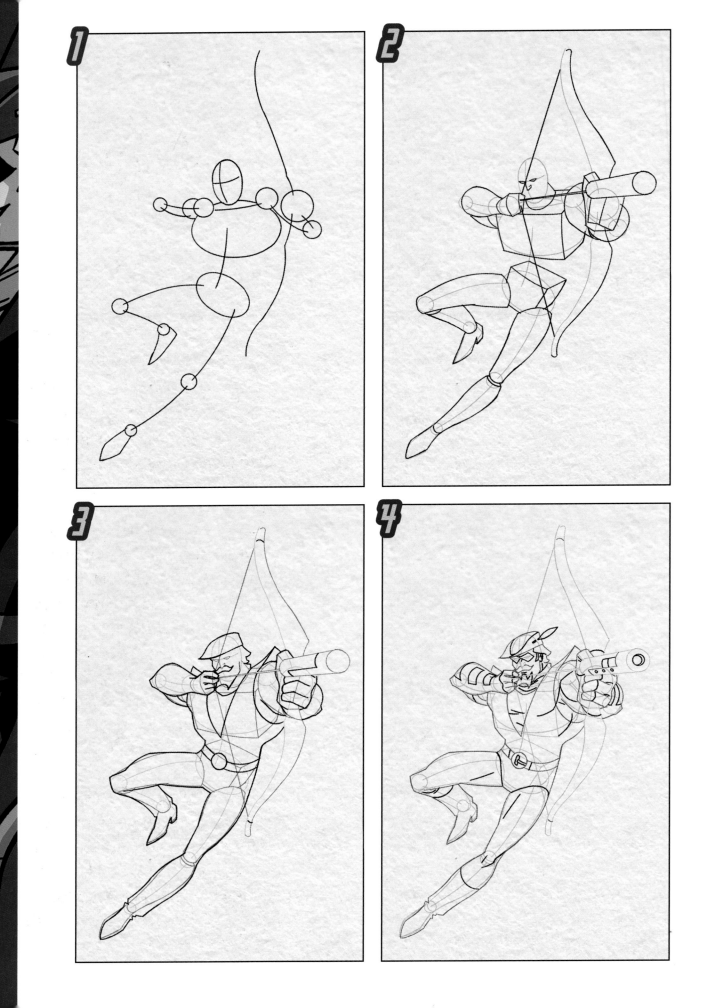

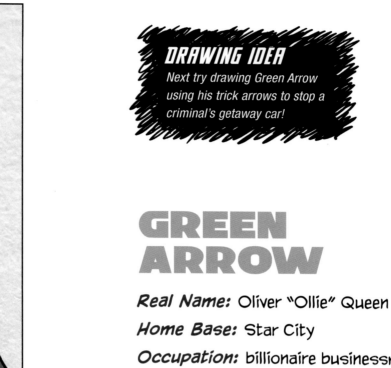

DRAWING IDEA
Next try drawing Green Arrow using his trick arrows to stop a criminal's getaway car!

GREEN ARROW

Real Name: Oliver "Ollie" Queen

Home Base: Star City

Occupation: billionaire businessman and politician, crime fighter

Abilities: expert marksmanship, hand-to-hand combat skills

Equipment: trick arrows

Background: As a boy Oliver Queen was skilled with a bow, and his hero was Robin Hood. When Ollie's parents were killed, he grew into a rich and spoiled thrill-seeker who cared only for himself. But that all changed one day when he was stranded on a small island. There he learned to survive by honing his fighting skills and becoming a master archer. After being rescued Oliver decided to change his ways. He now models himself after his childhood hero. He dresses in green and uses his amazing archery skills to keep crime off the streets of Star City.

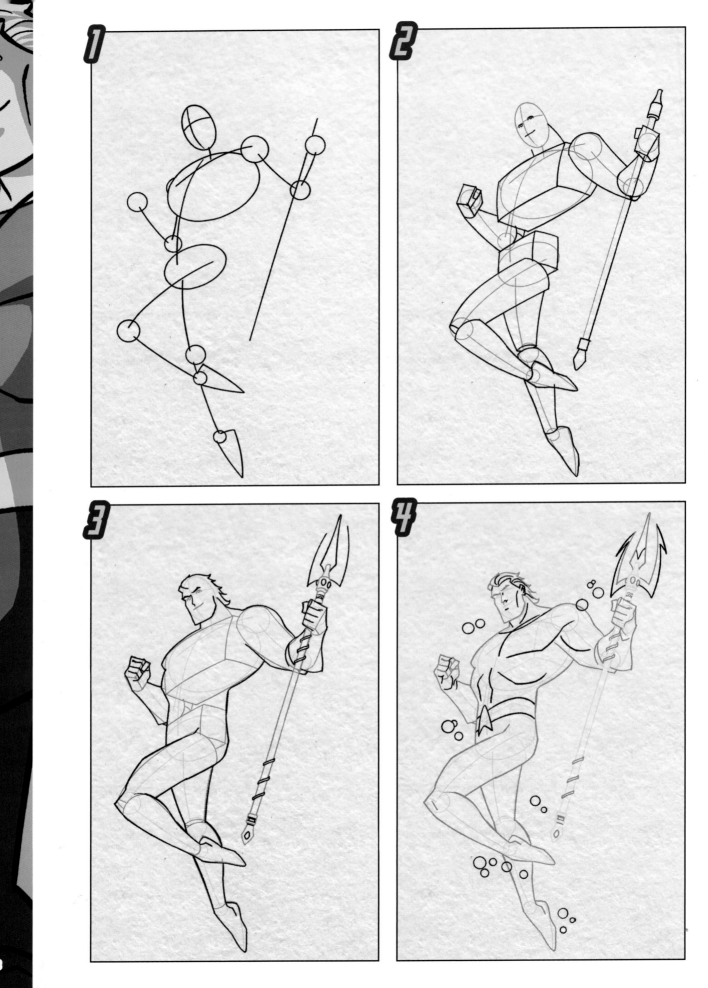

AQUAMAN

Real Name: Arthur Curry

Home Base: Atlantis

Occupation: King of Atlantis, protector of the oceans

Abilities: super-strength and speed, underwater breathing, telepathic communication

Background: Arthur Curry grew up as the son of a lighthouse keeper. At a young age, Arthur learned he could breathe underwater and talk to fish and other ocean animals. Eventually Arthur learned that his mother was the Queen of Atlantis and that he would one day be a king. When he grew up, Arthur decided to use his powers to defend the Earth's oceans and wildlife and help stop the world's worst villains.

DRAWING IDEA
Next try drawing J'onn J'onzz taking the shape of a powerful animal to help Green Lantern defeat Sinestro!

MARTIAN MANHUNTER

Real Name: J'onn J'onzz

Home Base: Mars, Justice League Watchtower

Occupation: detective, Martian police officer

Abilities: super-strength and speed, flight, telepathy, shape-shifting, investigation

Background: When powerful aliens invaded Mars, the Martian race was nearly wiped out. As the last survivor, J'onn J'onzz managed to escape and fled to Earth. There he joined Earth's mightiest heroes to defeat the alien threat. Afterward J'onn decided to make Earth his new home. Using his shape-shifting ability, J'onn blends in with Earth's people. He uses his telepathic powers and detective skills to solve crimes and stop villains' wicked plans.

CYBORG

Real Name: Victor "Vic" Stone

Home Base: Justice League Watchtower, Science and Technology Advanced Research (S.T.A.R.) Labs

Occupation: student athlete, crime fighter

Abilities: super-strength and speed, able to link with computers

Equipment: enhanced cybernetic systems

Background: Victor "Vic" Stone was visiting his father at the local S.T.A.R. Lab when he was horribly injured in an accident. Vic's father saved his life by replacing much of his body with cybernetic parts. Vic's new body gives him superhuman abilities, and he can link with almost any computer in the world. Vic once dreamed of becoming a star athlete. But now he has a new purpose—to fight crime as one of the world's greatest heroes.

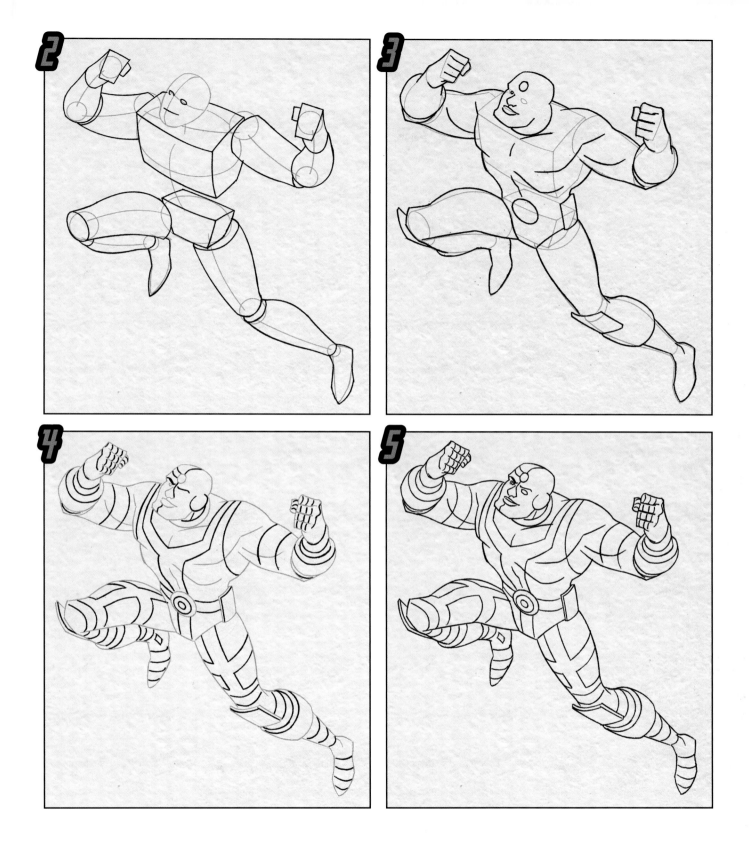

1

DRAWING IDEA
Next draw Black Canary using her special ability to help Green Arrow stop a bank robbery!

BLACK CANARY

Real Name: Dinah Lance

Home Base: Gotham City

Occupation: adventurer, crime fighter

Abilities: martial arts expert, ultrasonic Canary Cry scream

Background: Dinah Lance comes from a family of crime fighters. Her father is a police officer, and her mother fought crime as the original Black Canary. Her mother didn't want her to become a crime fighter, but Dinah followed in her mother's footsteps anyway. However, Dinah has a special ability of her own. Her ultrasonic Canary Cry scream can stun foes, damage objects, and even shatter metal!

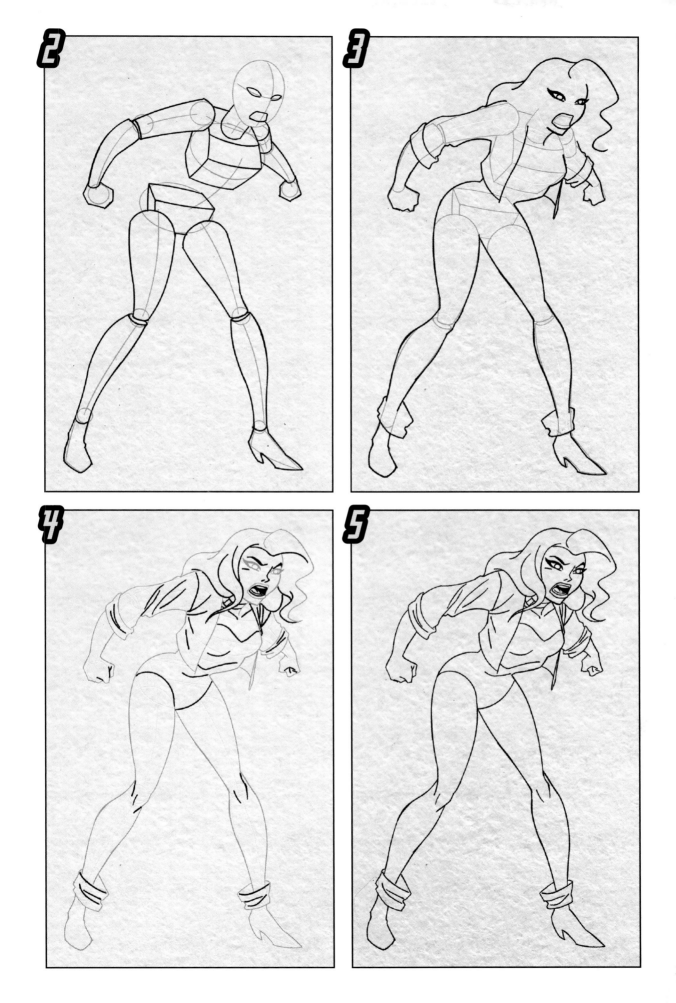

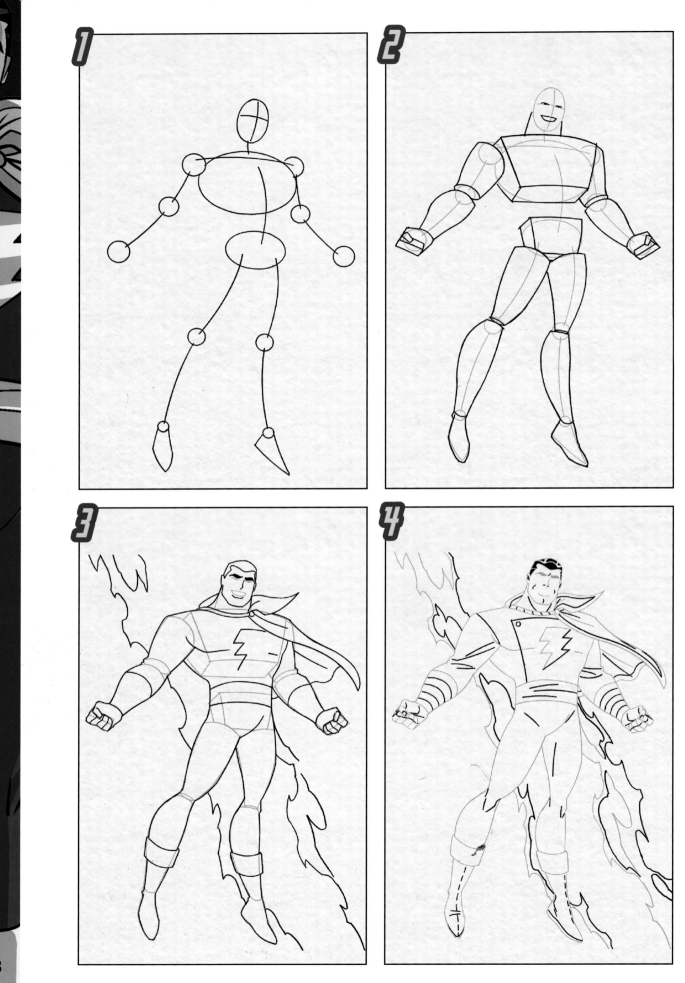

SHAZAM!

Real Name: William "Billy" Batson

Home Base: Fawcett City

Occupation: student, reporter, super hero

Abilities: super-strength, speed, and stamina; flight; invulnerability

Background: Young Billy Batson's parents were killed during an archaeology expedition in Egypt. The powerful wizard Shazam soon learned about Billy and his strong sense of justice. The wizard gave Billy the powers of several historical figures. These include the wisdom of Solomon, the strength of Hercules, the stamina of Atlas, the power of Zeus, the courage of Achilles, and the speed of Mercury. Now when Billy calls out the magic word "SHAZAM!," he is transformed into a mighty hero who is almost as powerful as Superman!

DRAWING IDEA
Try drawing SHAZAM! fighting his archenemy Black Adam to stop him from taking over the world!

HAWKMAN 1

Real Name: Carter Hall

Home Base: Midway City

Occupation: archaeologist and super hero

Abilities: enhanced strength and healing, flight

Equipment: Nth Metal wings, armor, and weapons

Background: While on a dig in Egypt, archaeologist Carter Hall discovered an ancient alien artifact. When he touched it, he received the memories of Katar Hol—a law officer from the planet Thanagar who had crash landed in ancient Egypt. After claiming the special Nth Metal wings, armor, and weapons that were nearby, Carter returned to Midway City. Now he patrols the skies there as the super hero Hawkman.

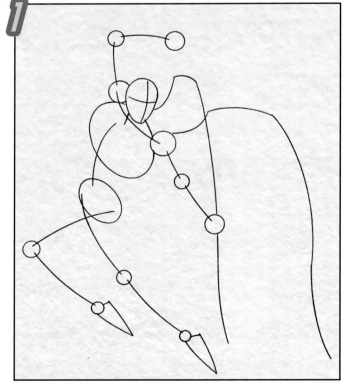

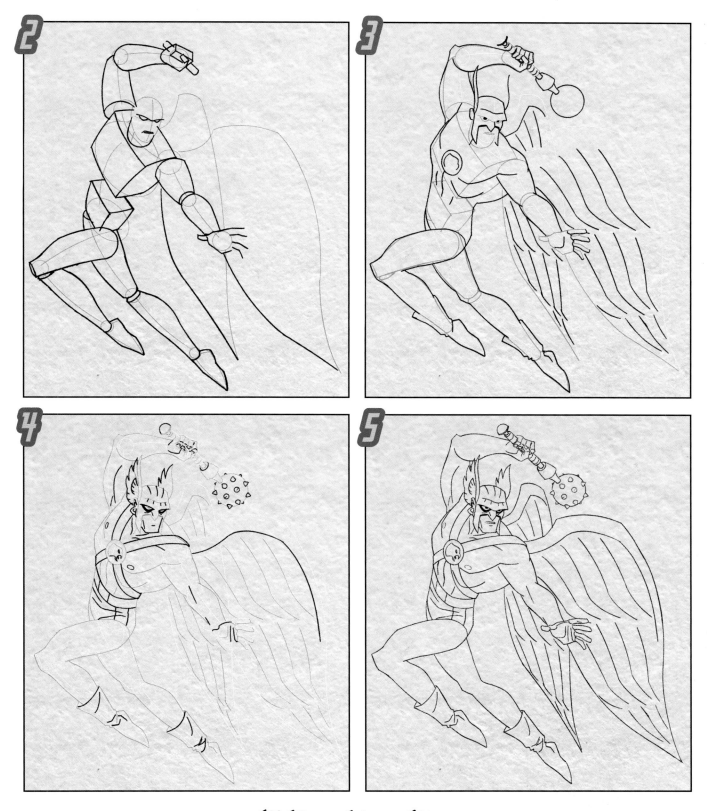

DRAWING IDEA
Next try drawing Hawkman fighting alongside Green Lantern to stop an alien invasion of Earth!

SUPERGIRL

Real Name: Kara Zor-El

Home Base: Metropolis

Occupation: student, super hero

Abilities: super-strength, speed, and hearing; X-ray vision; heat vision; flight; invulnerability

Background: Kara Zor-El is Superman's cousin and the last survivor of Krypton's Argo City. Like Kal-El, Kara was sent to Earth in a spacecraft. Superman took Kara to live with the Kents as their teenage niece. The Kents taught her the same values they had taught Clark. Meanwhile, Superman taught her how to control her newfound abilities. Eventually Kara moved to Metropolis to fight crime as Supergirl.

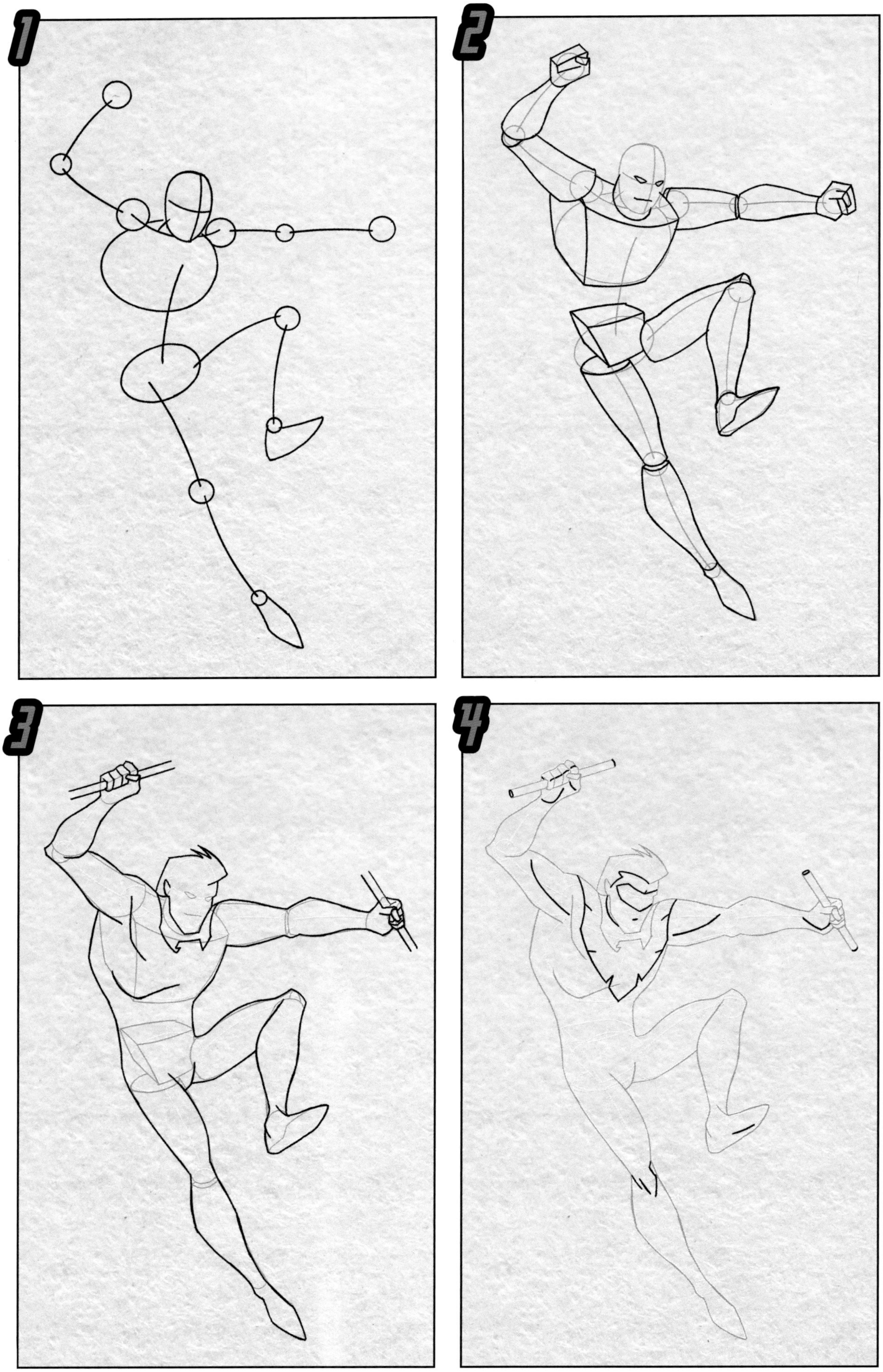
1
2
3
4

5

DRAWING IDEA
Now try drawing Nightwing using his acrobatic skills to take out a group of thugs on the street!

NIGHTWING

Real Name: Dick Grayson

Home Base: Blüdhaven

Occupation: adventurer, crime fighter

Abilities: master of martial arts and acrobatics, master detective

Equipment: pair of fighting sticks

Background: As a boy Dick Grayson was a member of the Flying Graysons, a family of circus acrobats. When Dick's parents were killed in a tragic accident, Bruce Wayne took in the heartbroken boy. When Dick learned that Bruce was secretly Batman, he began training to become the first Robin. Batman and Robin spent several years fighting crime together as the Dynamic Duo. But when Dick grew up, he struck out on his own. He created a new suit for himself and moved to a new city. Now he protects the streets of Blüdhaven as the acrobatic crime fighter, Nightwing.

THE JUSTICE LEAGUE

When Earth was invaded by powerful aliens, even the world's mightiest heroes were unable to defeat them on their own. Only by joining together did they have the strength to overcome the alien threat. After stopping the invasion, Superman, Batman, Wonder Woman, Green Lantern, The Flash, and Martian Manhunter formed the Justice League. The heroes then built the Watchtower, a space station that orbits the Earth. From here the Justice League can watch over Earth and launch powerful defenses to protect its people.

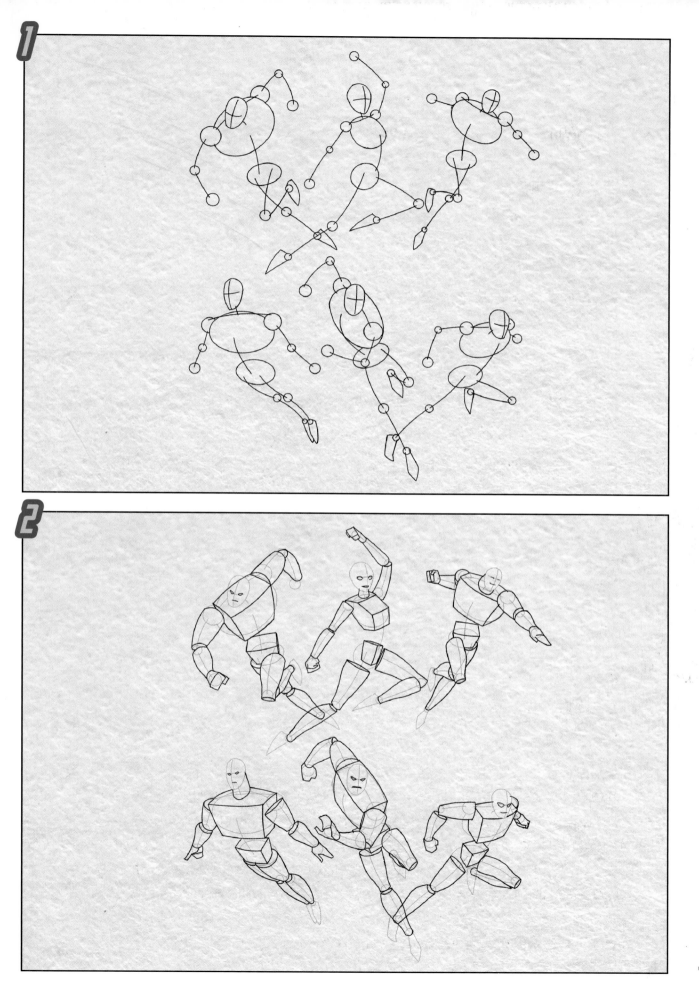

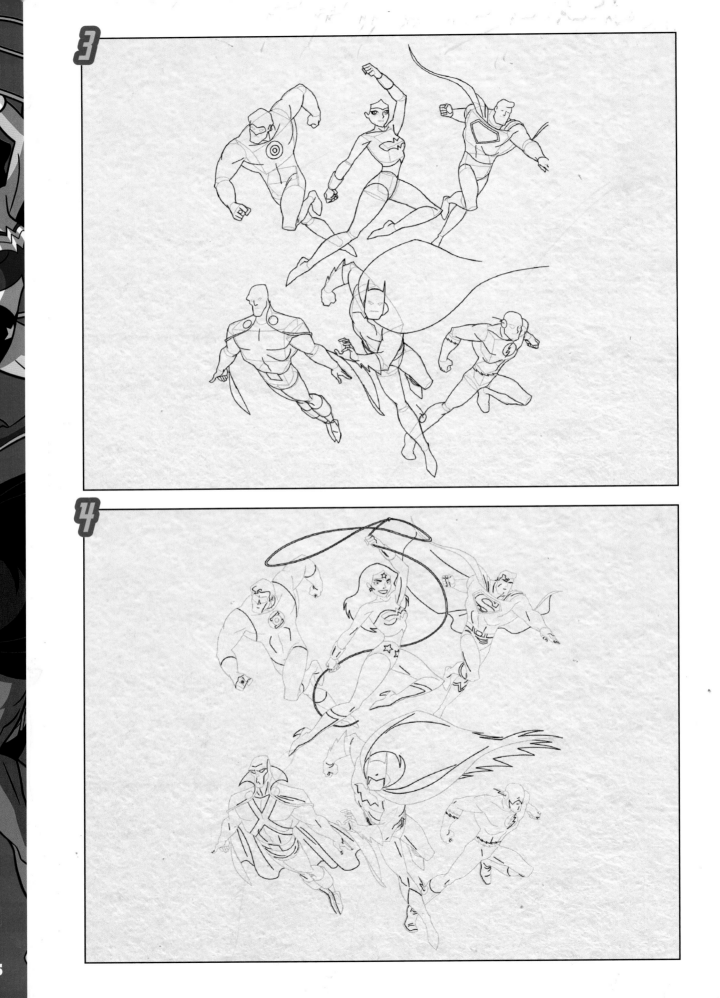

CHAPTER 4
DC SUPER-VILLAINS

What would Superman or Batman do if they didn't need to stop Lex Luthor or the Joker? How would Wonder Woman spend her time if she didn't have to fight Cheetah? Everybody loves super heroes. But the truth is, without super-villains to fight against, super heroes wouldn't have much to do.

Every super hero has a Rogues Gallery of villains to fight. Just like heroes, super-villains have a variety of powers, special abilities, and backgrounds. Some are super-intelligent humans. Others are powerful aliens. Some villains devise evil plans to get revenge on their archenemies. Others simply want to take over and rule the world. But villains all have one thing in common—they give us a reason to cheer for our favorite super heroes!

Welcome to the world of DC Super-Villains! Jump right in to begin sketching several fearsome villains such as Sinestro, Cheetah, and Black Manta.

Unleash your imagination and see what happens when your favorite heroes clash with these sinister super-villains!

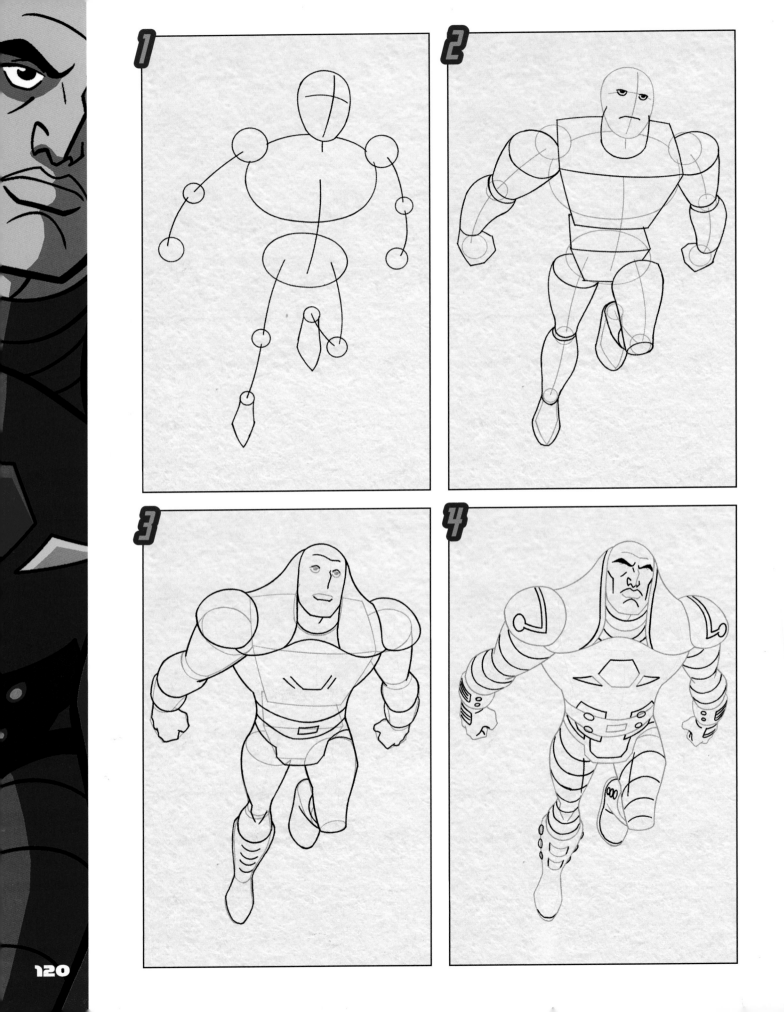

BATTLE ARMOR LEX

Real Name: Lex Luthor

Home Base: LexCorp, Metropolis

Occupation: successful businessman, criminal mastermind

Enemy of: Superman

Abilities: scientific genius

Equipment: Kryptonite battle suit

DRAWING IDEA
Try drawing Lex battling Superman in his armor high over Metropolis!

Background: Lex Luthor is one of Metropolis' richest and most powerful people. Behind the scenes he is a criminal mastermind and a scientific genius. To deal with Superman, Lex built a Kryptonite-powered battle suit. The armored suit gives him super-strength and allows him to fly. It's also armed with powerful Kryptonite energy weapons. While wearing his special battle suit, Lex is nearly a match for Superman.

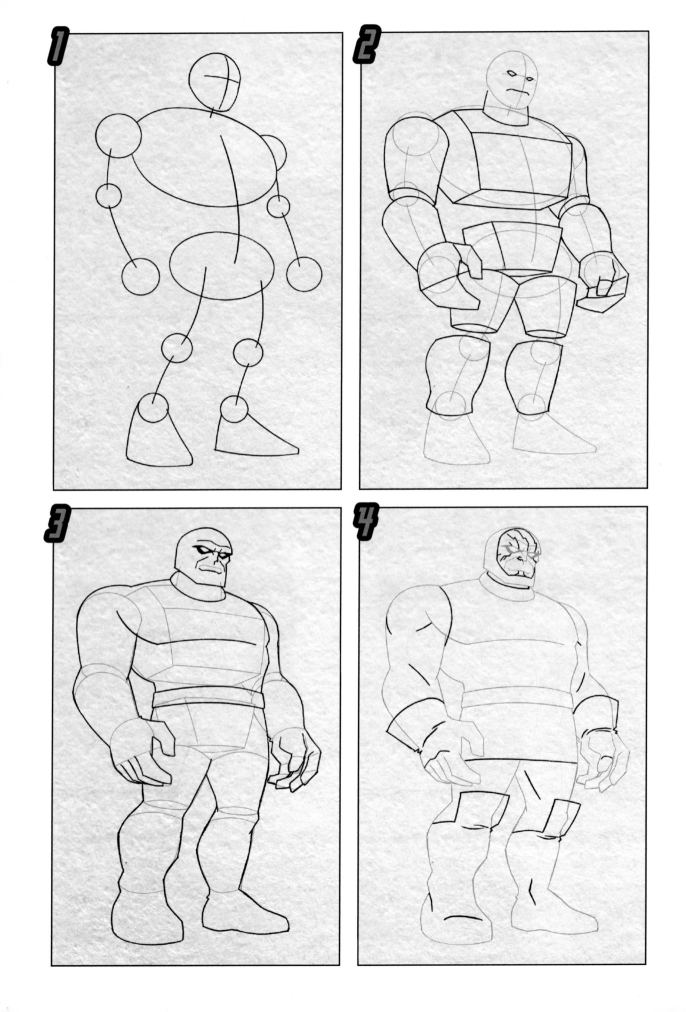

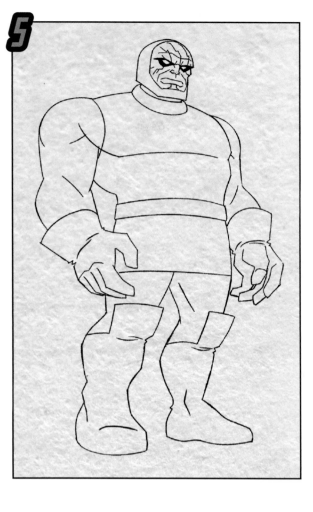

5

DARKSEID

Real Name: Uxas

Home Base: Apokolips

Occupation: dictator and tyrant, New God

Enemy of: Superman

Abilities: super-strength, speed, and stamina; invulnerability; immortality; genius intellect; telepathy; mind control; Omega Beams

Background: Darkseid rules over the planet Apokolips with an iron fist. But he also aims to rule the entire universe! Darkseid has limitless strength and can blast his enemies with deadly Omega Beams from his eyes. Only Superman has the strength to truly weaken or injure him. With his unmatched power, Darkseid is nothing less than the most dangerous enemy in the known universe.

DRAWING IDEA
Next draw Darkseid as he tries to defeat the Man of Steel with his deadly Omega Beams!

DRAWING IDEA

Try drawing Mr. Freeze stopping Batman in his tracks with his freeze gun!

MR. FREEZE

Real Name: Dr. Victor Fries

Home Base: Gotham City

Occupation: scientist, professional criminal

Enemy of: Batman

Abilities: enhanced strength, genius intellect

Equipment: cryo-suit, freeze gun

Background: One day scientist Victor Fries was accidentally soaked with chemicals in his lab. The accident changed his body so he could live only at sub-zero temperatures. To survive Victor built a special suit that keeps his body cold and gives him superhuman strength. To get the diamonds needed to power his suit, Victor turned to a life of crime. Calling himself Mr. Freeze, he uses a special freeze gun to aid him in his criminal activities.

THE PENGUIN

Real Name: Oswald Cobblepot

Home Base: Gotham City

Occupation: professional criminal

Enemy of: Batman

Abilities: genius intelligence, numerous criminal connections

Equipment: trick umbrellas

Background: Oswald Cobblepot's waddling walk and beakish nose earned him the nickname of the Penguin. He is almost always protected by several hired thugs. The Penguin also owns a number of special umbrellas that hide a variety of deadly weapons. Among these are a machine gun, a flamethrower, a sword, small blades, and poison gas.

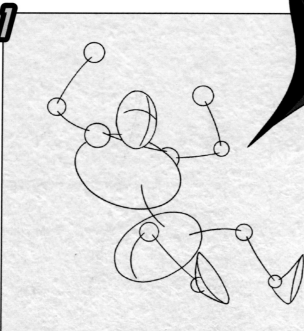

DRAWING IDEA

Next try drawing the Penguin using a special weapon umbrella to get away from Batman!

126

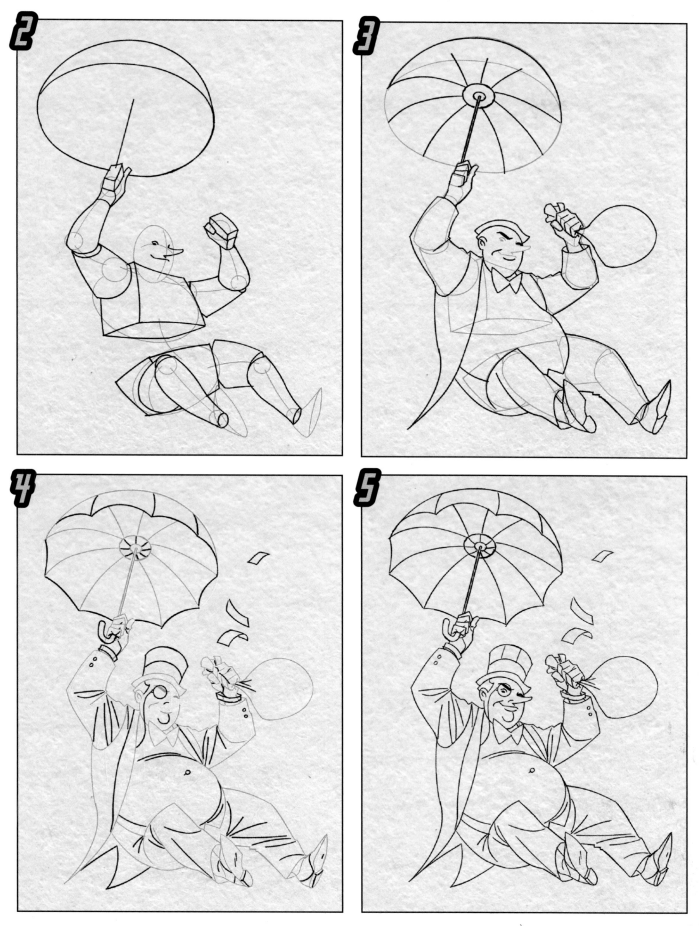

HARLEY QUINN

Real Name: Dr. Harleen Quinzel

Home Base: Gotham City

Occupation: psychiatrist, professional criminal

Enemy of: Batman

Abilities: Olympic-level gymnast and acrobat

Equipment: giant mallet

Background: Dr. Harleen Quinzel was once a successful psychiatrist at Gotham City's Arkham Asylum. But when she met the Joker, everything changed. When the Joker told Harley the heartbreaking, yet fake, story of his troubled childhood, her heart was won over. Harley fell in love with the Joker and soon helped him escape. She now clowns around Gotham City as Harley Quinn, the Joker's girlfriend and partner in crime.

DRAWING IDEA
Try drawing Harley and the Joker working together to set a deadly trap for Batman and Robin.

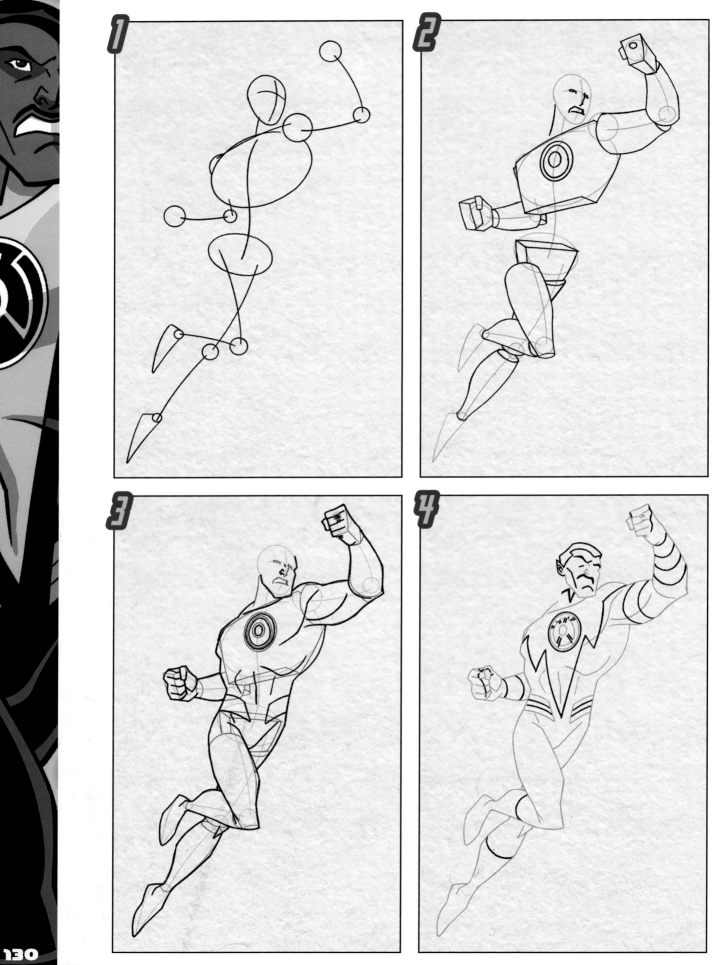

SINESTRO

Real Name: Thaal Sinestro

Home Base: Korugar, Qward

Occupation: Yellow Lantern

Enemy of: Green Lantern Corps

Abilities: military command, hand-to-hand combat skills, genius intellect

Equipment: yellow power ring

Background: Originally from the planet Korugar, Thaal Sinestro was once a famous member of the Green Lantern Corps. But he later turned evil and became a dictator over his home planet. Sinestro was eventually captured and banished to the planet Qward. However, he later obtained a yellow power ring that was just as powerful as the Lanterns' green rings. Sinestro then formed the Sinestro Corps and swore to get his revenge against the Green Lanterns.

DRAWING IDEA
Next try drawing Sinestro creating a powerful weapon with his yellow ring to fight Green Lantern!

DRAWING IDEA

Now try drawing Cheetah fighting
Wonder Woman with her catlike
reflexes and razor-sharp claws!

CHEETAH

Real Name: Barbara Ann Minerva

Home Base: Nottingham, United Kingdom

Occupation: biologist, professional criminal

Enemy of: Wonder Woman

Abilities: catlike agility and reflexes, enhanced strength and speed, night vision, razor-sharp claws

Background: Dr. Barbara Ann Minerva was a biologist working on advanced genetics research. One day she decided to test her research on herself. But she was transformed into a half-human, half-cheetah hybrid. She was soon considered a freak by her fellow scientists and others. Cheetah then turned to a life of crime. She is cunning and clever, and her catlike abilities make her a dangerous foe for Wonder Woman.

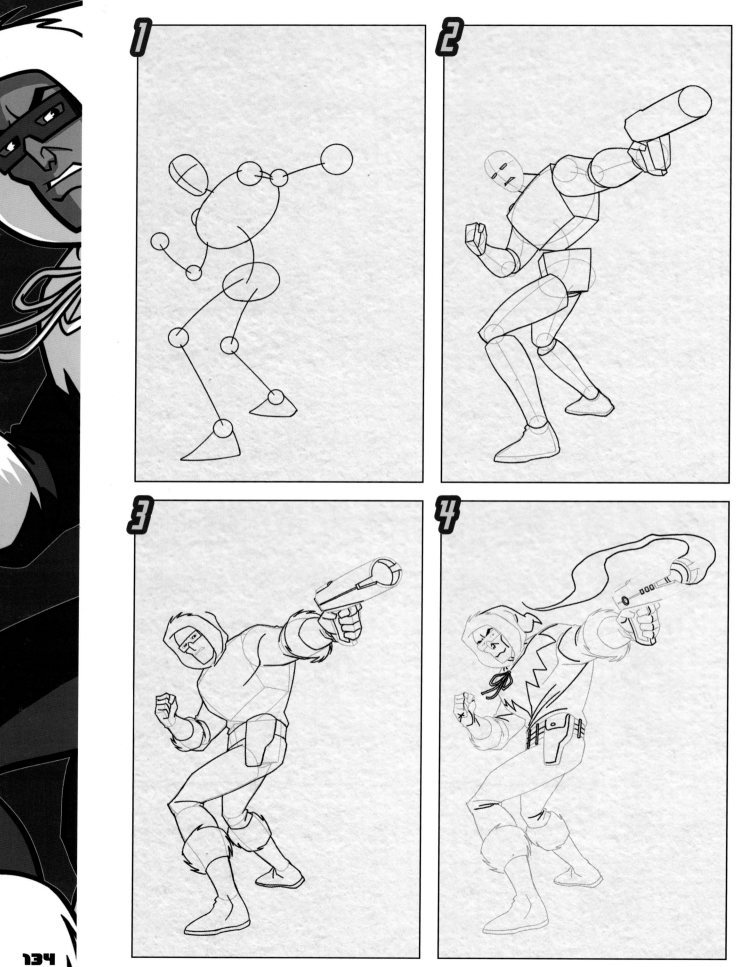

DRAWING IDEA
Now draw Captain Cold trying to blast The Flash with his powerful ultra-cold cannon!

CAPTAIN COLD

Real Name: Leonard Snart

Home Base: Central City

Occupation: professional criminal

Enemy of: The Flash

Abilities: skilled marksman, excellent strategist

Equipment: cold gun

Background: Captain Cold's name serves him well. He has nerves of ice and his cold heart helps him stay cool and collected in any situation. His special cold gun can instantly freeze objects into solid ice. Captain Cold also created an ultra-cold cannon that can bring even The Flash to a standstill. Now he looks for his chance to put the Scarlet Speedster on ice for good!

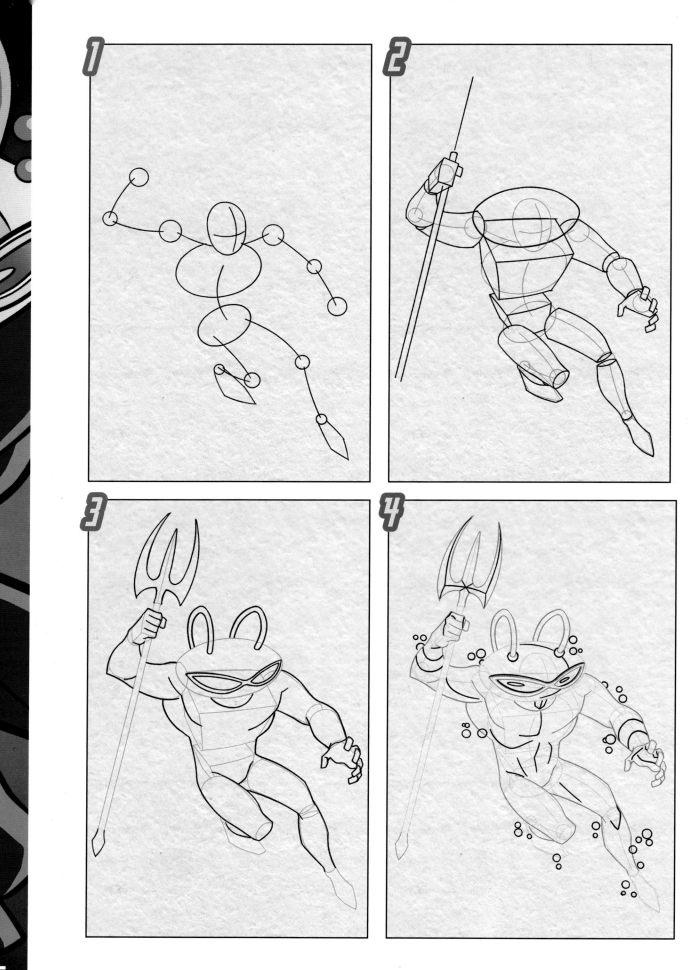

BLACK MANTA

Real Name: unknown

Home Base: the Ocean

Occupation: treasure hunter, assassin

Enemy of: Aquaman

Abilities: above-average strength and speed

Equipment: advanced diving suit, jet boots, miniature torpedoes, power helmet with infrared vision and energy beams

Background: As a young boy Black Manta was kidnapped and imprisoned on a small ship. One day he saw Aquaman and called out for help, but the Sea King didn't hear him. At that moment the boy swore to get revenge on Aquaman. When he finally escaped, he designed a high-tech diving suit and helmet. Now Black Manta has two goals—to destroy Aquaman and become ruler over the seas.

DRAWING IDEA
Try drawing Black Manta in an underwater brawl against Aquaman and his sea creature friends!

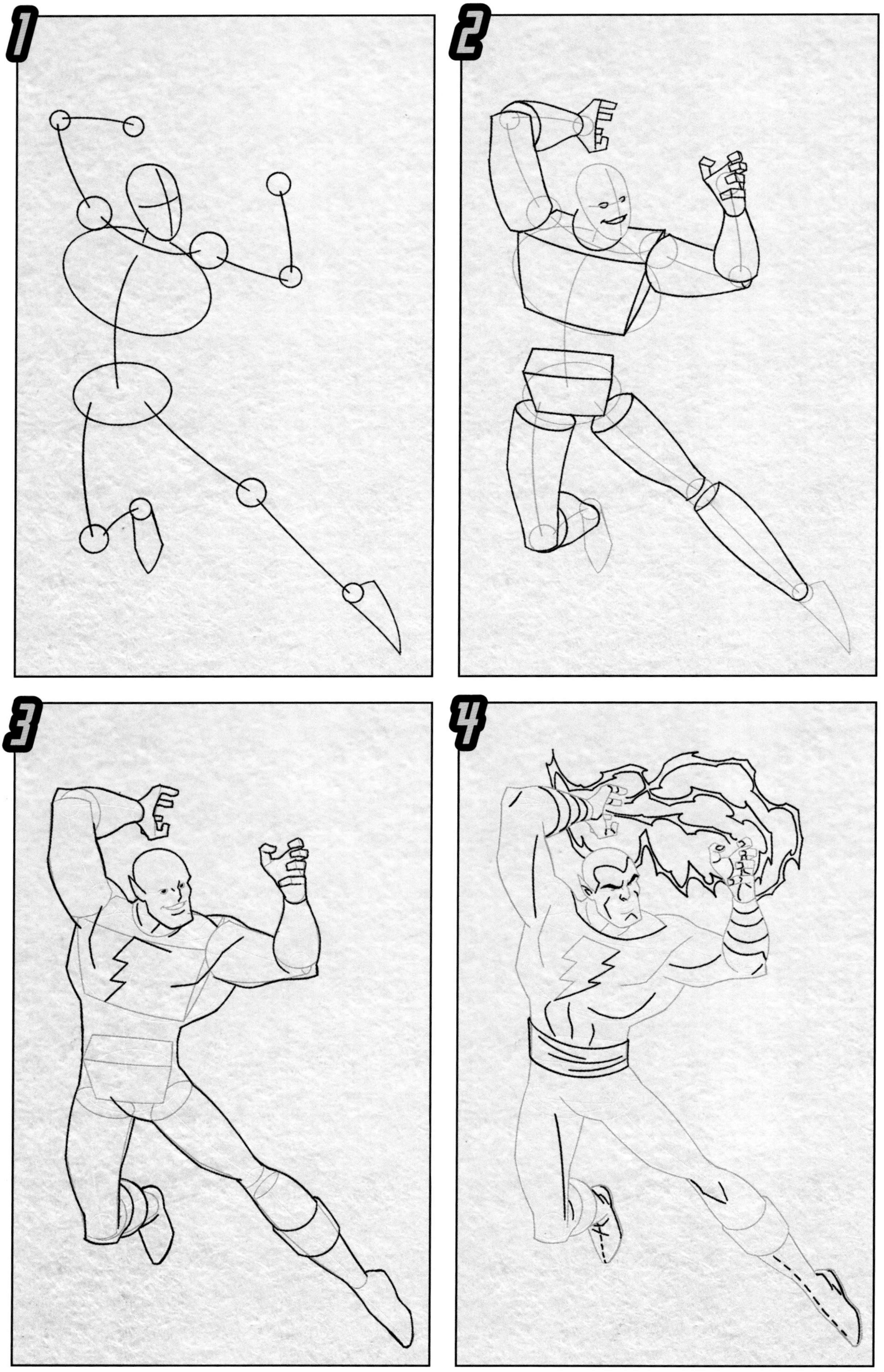
1
2
3
4

5

BLACK ADAM

Real Name: Teth-Adam

Home Base: Kahndaq

Occupation: dictator

Enemy of: SHAZAM!

Abilities: super-strength, speed, and stamina; enhanced intelligence; accelerated healing; flight; invulnerability

DRAWING IDEA
Try drawing Black Adam using his magical powers to battle his archenemy SHAZAM!

Background: Teth-Adam was once a fair and honest prince. The wizard Shazam gave him the powers of the gods Shu, Heru, Amon, Zehuti, Aton, and Mehen. But Adam later became a cruel dictator. Eventually, the wizard trapped Adam's soul and powers in a magic necklace. However, the necklace was later discovered by Adam's descendant, Theo Adam. Now Black Adam's powers and memories live on through Theo. Only SHAZAM! can stop the super-villain's goal of ruling the world.

SUPER-VILLAINS UNITED

Super-villains usually like to work alone. However, being a successful criminal can be difficult with super heroes around. To get an advantage, villains sometimes form secret groups to fight their enemies together. These groups have gone by several names including the Secret Society of Super-Villains, the Injustice League, and the Legion of Doom. Villains can be powerful and dangerous when they team up. But luckily, villains have a fatal flaw—they usually don't work well together. They often end up fighting one another instead of the heroes they hate!

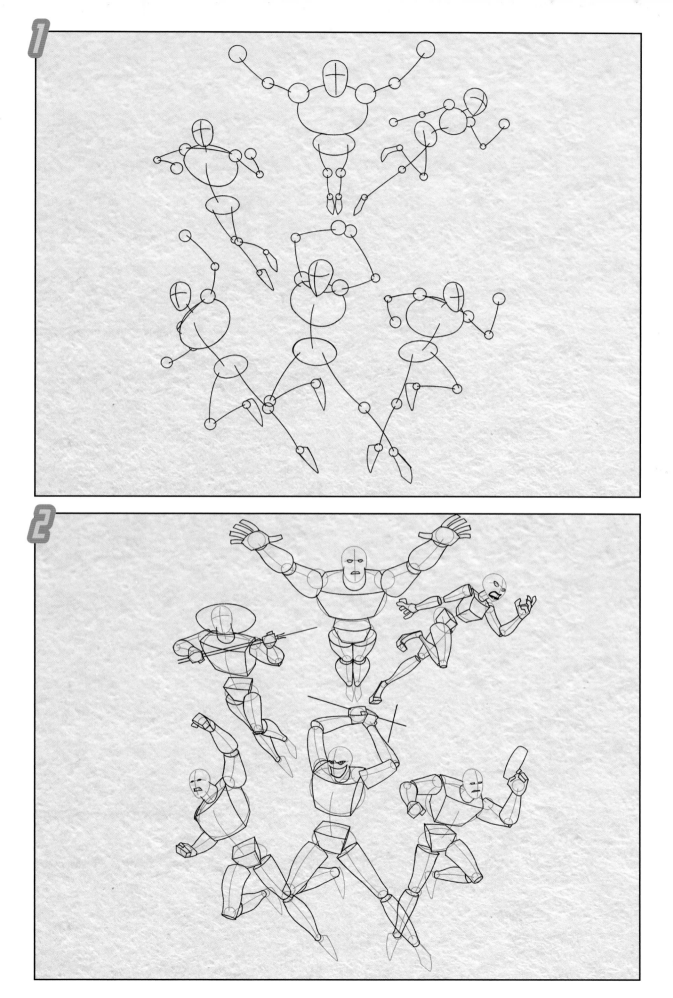

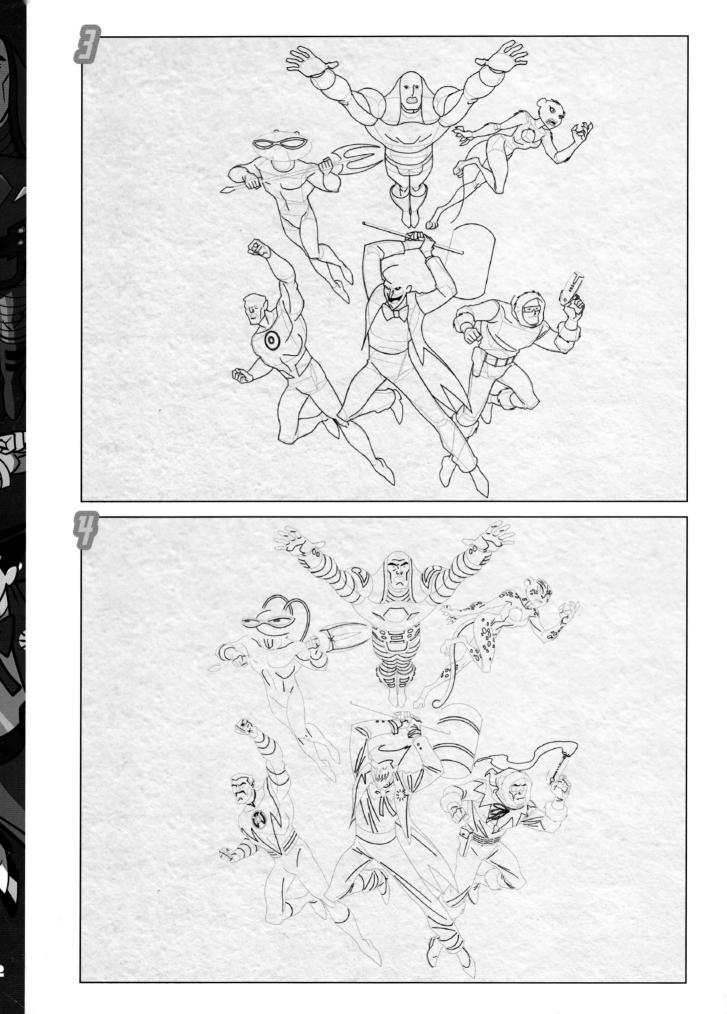

Published by Capstone Young Readers
1710 Roe Crest Drive
North Mankato, Minnesota 56003
www.capstoneyoungreaders.com

Library of Congress Cataloging-in-Publication Data

How to draw Batman, Superman, and other DC super heroes and villains /
by Aaron Sautter, illustrated by Erik Doescher and Tim Levins.
pages cm
Summary: "Step-by-step instructions teach readers how to draw DC super heroes
and their friends and enemies"—Provided by publisher.
ISBN 978-1-62370-231-1 (paperback)
1. Cartoon characters—Juvenile literature. 2. Superheroes in art—Juvenile literature.
3. Supervillains in art—Juvenile literature. 4. Drawing—Technique—Juvenile literature. I. Title
NC1764.8.H47S279 2015
741.5′1—dc23   2014023860

Editorial Credits

Ted Williams, designer; Kathy McColley, production specialist

Design Elements

Capstone Studio: Karon Dubke; Shutterstock: Artishok, Bennyartist, Eliks, gst,
Mazzzur, Roobcio

For Daniel and Isabelle — the coolest super heroes I'll ever know!
– A. Sautter

Printed in China.
092014   008474RRDS15